DIVINE AND HUMAN

DIVINE AND HUMAN

by

E. L. ALLEN

Ph.D., D.D.

Head of the Department of Divinity
King's College
Newcastle upon Tyne

LONDON : THE EPWORTH PRESS

Published by

THE EPWORTH PRESS

(FRANK H. CUMBERS)

25–35 City Road, London, E.C.1

*

| *New York* | . | *Toronto* |
| *Melbourne* | . | *Capetown* |

230V
Aℓ53

119137

First published in 1952

PRINTED IN GREAT BRITAIN
BY WESTERN PRINTING SERVICES LTD., BRISTOL

PREFACE

The substance of this book was originally given as four lectures to a Baptist ministers' retreat at Kent's Bank in February 1949. The kindly reception accorded to the lectures encouraged me to publish them, and they have benefited considerably in revision from suggestions and criticisms then received. I have endeavoured to find a new language in which to express the central Christian truths, a restatement of doctrine that does not betray it but rather makes it more convincing for our day. How far I have succeeded in this it will be for the reader to judge.

Acknowledgement is made to the Oxford University Press for permission to quote from Pedersen's *Israel: Its Life and Culture* and Alexander Dru's translation of Kierkegaard's *Journals*, to Messrs T. & T. Clark for a passage from H. R. Mackintosh's *The Doctrine of the Person of Jesus Christ*, to the Lutterworth Press for two from Harold Knight's *The Hebrew Prophetic Consciousness*, to the S.P.C.K. for one from *Reformation Old and New*, to Messrs. Allen & Unwin for one from Hartmann's *Ethics*, to the S.C.M. Press for one from Brunner's *God and Man*, and to the Philosophical Library, New York for two quotations from Martin Buber's *Hasidism*.

I am particularly indebted to my colleague, Dr G. H. Boobyer, who read and criticized the lectures in typescript before they were delivered, and who has helped in the reading of the proofs.

E. L. ALLEN

King's College
Newcastle upon Tyne

Contents

Chapter Four — MEDIA OF REVELATION

Chapter One

God and Man

I THE QUESTION

IT WAS A fateful moment in the history of the Hebrew tribes when, menaced by the superior armaments and the imperial ambitions of their Philistine neighbours, they drew together and resolved upon a king. Of what happened then two divergent accounts have come down to us. In one, the institution of the monarchy renews the mercy of the Exodus; again, as of old, God hears the cry of His oppressed people and sends them a man to be their deliverer. In the other, it is shameful error and rank apostasy, a human king is an upstart who invades the prerogatives of Israel's divine and only true lord.

It is possible to explain the difference between the two sources which have been laid under contribution by the compiler of 1 Samuel by dating one nearer to the event and the other at a distance from it. The hopes raised by Israel's entry upon Statehood gave way at a later period to disillusionment, especially in the prophetic circles which valued the nation's mission more highly than its power. But there is more to it than that. As we read the chapters in question, we are listening in to a debate in which opposite sides are being taken on one of the most fundamental issues for religious thinking.

The point in dispute is that of the relation between the divine and the human. For one source, the human is the medium of the divine self-expression, for the other God and man are opposed, and he who has the one must disavow the other. Once we see what is at stake, we are

9

driven to take sides ourselves. One of our ablest exponents of the Barthian theology has brought the ancient controversy up to date:

'The main theological issue today lies between those who hold by Calvin, called neo-Calvinists, and those who hold by Aquinas, called neo-Thomists. Is God the Lord, as Calvin maintains, transcendent, holy, separated from the world's sin by a gulf so great that it can only be bridged by Divine Grace? Or is there a continuity, and likeness, an *analogia entis*, between Creator and creature, even in his fallen condition, as Aquinas maintains? Thomism, and with it the whole Roman Catholic Church, holds that a natural knowledge of God by man is made possible even in his fallen state. Man is a rational animal, his nature is good, though not wholly good. But it has been spared a radical crisis. The bridge between God and man may be frail, but it remains unbroken. The supernatural can be reared upon the natural. As Aquinas puts it: "*Gratia non tollit sed perfecit naturam.*"'[1]

That, of course, is how a neo-Calvinist sees the situation. The neo-Thomist perspective might be a very different one. But there is a clear contrast between those for whom the God-man relation is positive and those for whom it is negative. Between the two we must choose. Or should we perhaps say that, being what we are and with all our experience of God's dealing with us in life, one of the two alternatives will be immediately convincing, so that we shall attach ourselves to it without questioning?

There is, however, a line of argument which is worth consideration. If we return in thought for a moment to the story in 1 Samuel from which we set out, we shall find that the antithesis with which it commences is not maintained in the sequel. It transpires that for the writer who does not approve of Saul, there *is* a human intermediary

[1] John McConnachie, in *Reformation Old and New* (1947), pp. 114f.

through whom God works. He is Samuel. Saul is cen-
sured because he does not give unconditional and even
unreasoning obedience to the word of the Lord by him.
The word of the Lord it is, but it is spoken by human lips.
Further, when Saul has been deposed for insubordina-
tion, Samuel is charged to anoint in his place the shepherd-
lad David as the man after God's own heart. So it is
possible after all for a man—and a king at that!—to be
used by God for the achievement of His purpose. Our
author does not object to a human king, but only to Saul
as such. It is not then a question of God *versus* man, but of
the particular man whom God chooses. In other words,
the negative view of the divine-human relationship in the
last resort presupposes the positive view. In precisely the
same way, the theologian who today objects to the intru-
sion of philosophy upon the preserves of theology turns
out on closer examination to have a favourite philosophy
of his own.[2]

But can we now explain the origin of the negative view
and the hold which it has over so many minds? For this,
we must have recourse to what I have urged elsewhere,
that any study of the prophets, if it is to be complete,
must include the men as well as their messages.[3] Isaiah
may bid us 'cease . . . from man, whose breath is in his
nostrils: for wherein is he to be accounted of?' (2^{22}).
But the very existence of an Isaiah compels us to account
highly of man. For Amos, there was nothing in Israel that
was worth preserving. We can see that there was. There
was Amos himself. He who, blinded by the vision of
God's transcendent majesty, speaks of Him with trembling
lips as 'Wholly Other'—are not his inspiration, his
insight into the divine purpose, and his passion for the
divine righteousness evidence enough to after generations

---

[2] On this see Daniel D. Williams on 'Barth and Brunner in Philosophy'
in the *Journal of Religion* (October 1947). [3] *Prophet and Nation* (1947).

that there is a spiritual kinship between God and man? In all these cases 'the transcendence of God is explicit; the immanence of God is implicit. But the whole revelation through prophecy rests on the assumption that human experience and thought *can* reveal God, which means that there is no fundamental unlikeness between the human and the divine personality.'[4]

II   CREATION

In any analysis of what is involved in the relation between the divine and the human, our starting-point is in the fact of creation. He who utters that word 'creation' sees a fathomless abyss opening at his feet. He stands on one side as the creature, while on the other God stands as the Creator. We are wholly dependent on Him, while He is wholly independent of us. The relation between the two is unique and is not adequately expressed even when we say that One is the Giver of life and the other the recipient of it. For in all our experience there is a self already there to do the receiving and all that happens is that something extra is added. But here the self is constituted in the very act of receiving; in the last resort, we have been given to ourselves by God.

Man shares therefore in this one-sided relation between God and what He has called into being. It may pass, but He remains. 'Lift up your eyes to the heavens, and look upon the earth beneath: for the heavens shall vanish away like smoke, and the earth shall wax old like a garment, and they that dwell therein shall die in like manner: but my salvation shall be for ever, and my righteousness shall not be abolished' (Isaiah 51[6]).

[4] H. W. Robinson: *Two Hebrew Prophets* (1948), p. 21. So, in reading the New Testament, it should not be forgotten that those who declare that the kingdom of God is for Him, and Him alone to bring, are at the same time giving their lives for its coming.

Though earth and man were gone,
And suns and universes ceased to be,
And Thou wert left alone,
Every existence would exist in Thee.

There is not room for Death,
Nor atom that his might could render void:
Thou—THOU art Being and Breath,
And what THOU art may never be destroy'd. [5]

Another consequence of what we have called the one-sided relation between Creator and creature is the rejection of any image, any object drawn from the created world, as a representation of God. To adopt such an image would be to shut one's eyes to the unbridgeable gulf which separates God from the world. It is noteworthy that the most vehement repudiation of images is to be found in Second Isaiah, the prophet in whose thinking the doctrine of creation is central and who set its peculiar stamp upon the word *bārā*. The expostulation, 'To whom then will ye liken me, that I should be equal to him? saith the Holy One' (Isaiah 40[25]), is set in the midst of what is surely the most magnificent description of the unrivalled majesty of God that is to be found in all literature. Since everything here below borrows its being from Him, there is nothing that can be accepted for a moment as an equivalent or a substitute for Him.

There is a word which describes the contingent and transitory nature of all that has thus issued from the hands of God, man included. It is the word 'flesh'. 'Flesh' stands for weakness, dependence, fragility, mortality—and all these are characteristic of man. In virtue of these he is identified with the brute creation, for all that has life is also flesh. 'All flesh is grass, and all the goodliness thereof is as the flower of the field: the grass withereth,

[5] Emily Brontë: *Last Lines.*

the flower fadeth; because the breath of the Lord bloweth upon it: surely the people is grass' (Isaiah 40 [6f.]). In the ever-memorable words, 'Now the Egyptians are men, and not God; and their horses flesh, and not spirit' (Isaiah 31 [3]), man is situated in the world of the transitory and perishable over against the world of the ever-living and the ever-mighty. 'Man is flesh and therefore cannot set himself up against God; it is foolish to trust in man instead of in God. . . . The fact that the souls of men are flesh is why the soul of God cannot commune directly with them. But, on the other hand, it is the idea that man "is but flesh, a breath that passeth away and cometh not again" which rouses the pity of God and makes him forgive his sins' (Psalm 78 [39]). [6]

That is the sobering aspect of the relation between the Creator and the creature. But it is not the only one. In the Bible, it is just those writers who lay most emphasis on man's insignificance *over against* God who are most persuaded of his significance *under* God. That is particularly true of Second Isaiah. Israel's security is in 'the everlasting God, the Lord, the Creator of the ends of the earth' (40 [28]), as the Servant is sustained in his mission by Him who 'created the heavens' and 'spread abroad the earth' (42 [5]). Precisely because man is flesh, he is not to be feared. 'Fear ye not the reproach of men, neither be ye dismayed at their revilings. For the moth shall eat them up like a garment, and the worm shall eat them like wool' (51 [7f.]).

To sum up. Man is the creature whom God has made. Let him lose contact with the source from which he draws his being, and he becomes weak, vacillating, restless, dissatisfied, and futile. Let him return to God and there is no heroism of which he does not become capable. For God 'is the mirror which discloses to every creature its

[6] Pedersen: *Israel: Its Life and Culture*, I–II (1926), pp. 176f.

own greatness'.[7] But this theme demands separate treatment.

So far, we have been concerned solely with what man has in common with the rest of the creation. Like all else that lives and moves upon this earth, he is flesh. What is it then that is distinctive of man? In the terminology of the Bible, it is the fact that he is created 'in the image of God'. For the connotation of this term we must not, of course, confine ourselves to the priestly writer whose account of the origin of things stands on the first page of Genesis. Man is constituted as man, we may say, by his relation to God, by his capacity to have dealings with Him, to understand and serve His will. Such lordship over nature as he enjoys is derived from this, since he is over nature only because he is first under God. That is to say, nature does not stand at man's arbitrary disposal, it is a sphere of trust and moral accountability. That this is so should not be difficult for a generation to appreciate which is threatened with famine by its thoughtless misuse of the earth's resources. The essence of human nature is to be found in moral responsibility. Man not only is, he ought to be, something.

This view of what it means to be human is dynamic, it fixes attention on man's situation rather than on his native endowment. Human nature does not emerge from the hands of God a fixed and finished product. The popular maxim that 'you cannot change human nature' overlooks the fact that the capacity for change is of the very essence of human nature. The existentialist philosophy of our time has brought out that selfhood is rather a possibility than an actuality. I am what I have it in me to become.

[7] A. N. Whitehead: *Religion in the Making* (1926), p. 155.

> *Our destiny, our being's heart and home,*
> *Is with infinitude, and only there;*
> *With hope it is, hope that can never die,*
> *Effort, and expectation, and desire,*
> *And something evermore about to be.*

Man has his being, therefore, in the purpose and hope of God, who intends him for fellowship with Himself. He is not so much something which already is as 'something evermore about to be'. Once we cease to confine our attention to Genesis 1 and try to grasp the biblical conception of man as a whole, we see that this is so.

'Man has no divine soul-substance. He is not endowed with any fixed nature constitutive of his resemblance to God. He is a frail creature of dust, but he is capable of being used as a vehicle for the manifestation of the divine. The true end of his life is not deification, but the embodiment of a divine meaning. His uniqueness lies in his addressability by God, his capacity to receive and express in human terms the divine Word. It is precisely in his becoming vitally related to God through his responsive surrender to the divine demand that he actualizes his kinship with God and elicits the divine image within him.'[8]

Modern science has taught us to think of creation, not as an event in the remote past, but as something which is going on here and now. Is it not thus also with the making of man? Each individual, however accidental his arrival here, brings with him a fresh thought on the part of God, gives occasion for an unprecedented enterprise of the love whose highest aim is to fashion creatures capable of responding with love.

'The creativity of God is a continuous process, and

[8] Harold Knight: *The Hebrew Prophetic Consciousness* (1948), p. 126. See now Karl Barth: *Kirchliche Dogmatik*, III. 2.

man's distinctive prerogative among the creatures is seen in the fact that he does not come forth as a completed article from the divine workshop. His characteristic humanity does not reside in any irrevocably given faculty, but is something which can only be realized by living and dramatic intercourse with his Creator. His resemblance to God springs from his inalienable capacity for such dynamic fellowship.' [9]

Man therefore has a dignity and an opportunity which are his alone. God has a purpose in the making of the world, and that purpose He does not Himself carry to completion, He trusts the completion of it to man. In the great words of the mystic, it is given to each one of us to be to the Eternal what His hand is to a man.

But thereby hangs a peril. Man was created for fellowship with God. That fellowship can only be actualized in freedom. And man may use his freedom to reject that fellowship. He may sin. Now a dynamic view of human nature such as we have just sketched quite clearly commits us to an equally dynamic view of sin. We must, that is to say, give up the whole idea of a creation at one point in the past followed by a fall at another point in the past, separated from it by an interval. We must locate both in the present. If the reality of man lies, as we have suggested it does, in a capacity, in what he may become, in 'something evermore about to be', then we must say that he lives from moment to moment between the glorious possibility of likeness to God and the shameful possibility of estrangement from Him. The dramatic relationship between God and man thus becomes a tragic one. It is not that Adam once 'brought death into the world, and all our woe', but that each of us is continually doing so. Man, both as the individual and as the race, is for ever turning from the voice of God in his

[9] Harold Knight, op. cit., p. 127.

B

soul. Yet no necessity is laid upon him to do so, and the divine love does not cease to plead with him: 'Why will ye die?' Frail creature of dust as he is, man is burdened with a heavy responsibility and is elect to the highest order of nobility. If he so wills, he can accomplish the purpose for which the world was made. If he does not, he can frustrate it. Is not that precisely the spiritual situation in which we stand today? The atom's imprisoned energies have been released, and it is for us to decide whether this will bring an immense enlargement of happiness and freedom or will shatter Western civilization. And the horror of it is that we are falling, falling, falling.

For the present tense is here more appropriate than the past. Our temptation, our peril, and our surrender are in the present. To speak of man as fallen is to suggest that his fate is settled, that what he is he must remain. It is better therefore to speak of him as *falling*, and to bear in mind that we are not spectators of another's shame, that we are involved in that of which we speak. In the last resort, each one of us is 'the Adam of his own soul'.

The story in Genesis 3 is wrongly used when it is read as the narrative of a primal fault of whose consequences we, alas, have been made the victims. It is rather to be taken as a protest against all those evasions to which we so easily resort. It is like one of those diagrams in a text-book of physics, which simplify the problem by reducing it to bare essentials, even though the complexity of our world is such that it never presents itself to us in fact in anything like so tractable a form. Adam, as the first man, is man without heredity; in the earthly paradise, he is man without unfavourable circumstances. As such, he shows how sin enters the world by an act of freedom. It is the same with ourselves, though we have, as he had not, our heredity and our unfavourable circumstances. When every allowance has been made for these, the responsibility remains for the use of just that measure of freedom which is given to us. There is an inner realm in which our moral fate is decided—and it is we who decide it.

We are therefore not shut up, as it was suggested earlier that we are, to the choice between neo-Thomism and neo-Calvinism. Neither of them has had the courage to break with the scheme of a creation and a fall with a time-interval between them. What do we substitute for this? A single continuous activity of the living God and man's varying response to it. Within this three moments can be distinguished. The first is *creation*, God's unceasing endeavour to fashion creatures who can enter upon the glorious liberty of His children and who will meet His love with love of their own. The second is *sin*, man's failure, whether in the race or the individual, to rise to the height of his destiny, to respond to the divine appeal. The third is *redemption*, the renewed and unwearying effort on God's part still to achieve His purpose and our good, not to accept from us a thousand refusals but somehow at the last to win our consent and return.[10]

IV THE MEANING OF HISTORY

This divine discipline of man, the long and patient effort on the part of God to fulfil in him His original intention, takes place within the sphere of history. The

[10] 'Each moment of a person's life is really set between creation and redemption; it falls within creation in that it is made, it is tied and bound to redemption in virtue of its power for making; or rather, it is not so much set between the two as in both jointly. Just as creation did not take place once and for all at the beginning of time, but happens all the time throughout the whole of time, so redemption will not come to pass at the end of time, but happens all the time throughout the whole of time. The moment is not merely co-ordinated to creation and redemption, but creation and redemption are also contained in it.' Martin Buber: *Hasidism* (1948), pp. 110f.

Old Testament writers saw that clearly when they attempted, sometimes shortsightedly and sometimes again with inspired sensitiveness to the great issues involved, to interpret the changing fortunes of their people as a work of God with them. We too must raise the question of the meaning of history. To this question three answers of major importance have been given.

The first is that which has behind it centuries of Christian tradition and which is familiar to us all from the New Testament and our hymns. According to it, the meaning of history lies in its character as *probation*. Man is an immortal soul passing through this world and his home is not in it. It is the opportunity given him to choose what shall be his destination for eternity, heaven or hell. Something of the kind goes back, of course, as far as Plato's *Phaedo*, and in our own time expression has been given to something very reminiscent of it in Arnold Toynbee's Burge memorial lecture. [11]

With the modern period, however, it became impossible to maintain this devaluation of the present world by contrast with a future one. The meaning of history was therefore found in *progress*. We need not take too seriously the extravagant expectations of the perfectibility of man which were entertained by some of the French *philosophes*; it is common knowledge that no new truth is merely discovered, it is exaggerated at the same time. But clearly any attempt to assess the extent to which humanity as a whole has made progress is beyond us; we can only observe particular directions in which progress has been registered during the time for which we have records. Transport has developed, ever wider forms of political organization have been devised, the arts have a larger range of materials and techniques at their disposal, language has become an ever more delicate means of

[11] *Christianity and Civilization* (1940).

expression, and so on. There is manifestly progress in what man *has*. But we are left asking whether there is similar advance in what he *is*.

In our own time we have been seized by doubt precisely at this point, and there is a mood abroad for which history has no meaning at all.[12] Things just happen, they lead nowhere, and a general survey of the ages leaves on some minds only an impression of chronic futility. The pace of modern life is such that before we have solved one problem it has been replaced by another. We legislate against folly and men have recourse to vice. We create a system which obviates one evil only to produce a worse, as we come home from a war to save us from a tyranny of the Right to find that we are threatened by a still more formidable tyranny from the Left. Two deductions from such observations are possible and both are met with today. The first is the despair of the ordinary man, who either contracts out of political action altogether or puts a blind trust in those who govern his country, since otherwise he is lost. The second is the grim *credo* of the theologian, for whom man 'is cursed by a fatal contradiction which ordains that the power by which he advances in civilization nullifies and destroys his own progress'.[13] Or again, we are told that history 'decisively demonstrates the radical impotence of man in the moral realm of destiny'.[14]

This view of history begins by expelling God and leaving man to conduct a colossal endeavour entirely on his own resources. God condemns him in his failure and intervenes in forgiveness and regeneration with the offer of grace. The position adopted in these lectures is that history is the sphere of constant divine-human interaction,

[12] Spengler's cyclical view of history may be cited in this connexion, also the well-known passage in the preface to Fisher's *History of Europe*.
[13] D. R. Davies: *On To Orthodoxy* (1948), pp. 212f.
[14] D. R. Davies: *Theology and the Atomic Age* (1947), p. 27.

its inmost meaning is the divine endeavour to bring man to his true destiny and the possibility, from situation to situation, of man's co-operation with this work of love or his refusal of it. This means that if history is incomplete by man's sin it is also incomplete by God's wisdom. He intends that the basic human problem, the choice between good and evil, life and death, shall arise afresh in each generation. It is like an examination which each year has a different set of questions to answer, because it is an essential part of the test that no one should be able to get through merely by reproducing what his predecessors did.

We may picture history therefore as a spiral. To simplify our account, we abstract from the periods of retrogression which unquestionably occur and fix our attention upon those factors which show progress. As we climb such a spiral, we find again and again that, while we occupy a higher level, we are still over the point from which we set out. The tradition which accumulates and which gives us our national health service, our electric cookers, and our atom-bombs, does nothing to relieve us of the stark and dreadful responsibility which we share with all who went before us. We have more than they had, but the test of our worth is not in what we *possess*, but in what we *are*, in the use to which we put our possessions. Even where what we are is affected (e.g. when social changes make man more aware of himself as an individual), the basic ethical situation remains unchanged. If our temptations are in some respects less obvious than our fathers', in others they are more subtle. We must live under different circumstances, but to live means for us exactly what it meant for them— a meeting with the God who made us and in whose will is our peace. History is the continually changing setting in which He makes of us His unchanging requirement, that we should do justly, love mercy, and walk humbly in His sight.

Thus in a sense we return to the idea of probation. Only it is a probation of present character rather than of final destiny. History is a vale of soul-making rather than of soul-saving in the traditional sense of those words. This, however, carries with it an important consequence. If the examination which we sit in this world is one of character and not merely of knowledge, it follows that the tasks assigned to us must be real tasks, that what we are called to do must have worth in itself. You cannot truly measure a man's strength by telling him to dig a hole and then fill it in; you must give him something in which he perceives a value. If therefore we say, as we have done, that in the effort to create, maintain, and extend civilization generation by generation man is being tested to see whether he will choose the good and refuse the evil, we must go on to say that the labour of civilization is itself the will of God for men. The old story of the Tower of Babel must not mislead us. In the work of civilization man does not build merely out of pride. He builds out of need. Security, shelter, provision for the future and for those who cannot supply their own wants, forms of association which link together those who are separated and whose interests are diverse—it is the will of God that man should fashion such things. But how he does it and to what plan, and what life he lives in these structures when he has finished them—this also is what God requires of him. We serve God as we order and use that over which He has set us, and equally in so doing we find or miss our destiny as immortal selves.

But if the meaning of history is to be found within history, that is not true of the whole meaning. If personalities are created in and through the making of civilization as a task set to humanity by God, those personalities rise above that civilization and abide when it perishes. The function of death is twofold. It makes possible the entry of successive generations upon the exacting but noble enterprise of living, and it transfers the individual from a lower to a higher school of training. We find ourselves through application to social tasks, but the selves we find have a value which society does not possess. Only as we do justice both to the progress of the race and to the immortality of the person do we save ourselves from, in the one case, robbing this world of the values God set in it, and, in the other, sacrificing all generations to the one which reaches the goal of the classless society.

V   THE JUDGEMENT OF GOD

The distinctive attribute of the God who disciplines mankind in history is His holiness. One of the simplest ways of marking off holiness from its near neighbours, righteousness and goodness, is by noting the difference in the tone of voice when we pass to it from the other two. There is a suggestion of awe, of approaching something which may not be lightly handled, which evokes respect, reverence, and so on. Righteousness and goodness we may admire, but praise is vulgar and out of place where holiness is concerned. Conscience may claim the right to judge them, but by holiness it is itself rebuked and reduced to silent, all-surrendering homage. We feel that holiness should be absolute or should not be at all; it seems out of place to admit degrees in it, once we have understood what it means. It is therefore indefinable, but we can recognize it. God is where it is, and only in a secondary sense can it be applied to things human, as something which they borrow from Him.

Holiness now must be conceived dynamically; it reacts against sin in condemnation and repulsion. God is of purer eyes than to behold evil; holiness *is* this stark, uncompromising hostility to the bare suggestion of evil. There is something much more positive here than simply a retreat of good into a fastness where it is inaccessible to evil. That would be a very poor antagonism to evil which allowed it free course in the world provided one could only find somewhere in which to preserve one's purity from it. There is in holiness a principle of retribution, a wrath of God that is 'revealed from heaven against all ungodliness and unrighteousness of men' (Romans 1[18]). No doubt, as Professor Dodd has urged, there is good reason for supposing that by the time of Paul the wrath of God was no longer thought of as a violent, explosive emotion on His part, resentment against personal injury and so on. It has come to stand rather for the working of the law by which a man reaps as he has sown, a moral order of the universe.[15] There is a striking passage in Wisdom (18[20-5]) in which 'the wrath' has clearly become hypostatized in this way. It came forth from God in the first instance but has as it were become detached from Him.

We gain much by such an interpretation, but we lose not a little at the same time. The less personal the divine reaction against sin, the less hope is there that it may ever be reversed. The law which in the East rivets consequence to deed is independent of any god's displeasure. Yes, but for that very reason it goes on inexorably.

> *The Moving Finger writes; and, having writ,*
> *Moves on: nor all thy Piety nor Wit*
>   *Shall lure it back to cancel half a Line,*
> *Nor all thy Tears wash out a Word of it.*

You cannot ask a law or a principle to forgive you, only a person can do that. And before he can forgive he must

[15] *Romans* in Moffatt New Testament *Commentary* (1937), pp. 20ff.

in some way have been outraged. We like to say in these days that it is in the nature of things that sin brings suffering in its train. But whoever heard of the nature of things crying to men: 'Turn ye, why will ye die?' Here, as so often, we must use both types of expression. We must conceive the divine reaction against evil as a principle of retribution so as to purge it of any resemblance to our human anger. But if we want to keep open the possibility of forgiveness we must think of God as personally moved by what we do.

Can we now attempt a more adequate account of what is meant by the judgement of God upon human sin? We can if we take our cue from the pathetic life-story and heroic patience of Hosea. There is no need to retell his story here. It is sufficient to say that, faced with the disloyalty of his wife, he can neither abandon her nor condone what she has done. Therefore he decides upon a temporary separation, in the hope that this will give her time to reflect and so he will win her back. As he arrives at this singularly noble resolve, a glimpse is granted him into the very heart of God. He sees that when God judges Israel, as He is most certainly about to do, it will not be in anger but in sorrow, that with Him judgement is always and only an instrument of love. God proposes to part the nation from all that has been abused to infidelity in the past, from the ceremonial of religion and the policies of the State. Perhaps, when disaster falls upon the land, Israel will be reduced to the dimensions of a desert tribe once more. But in that return to her earliest conditions, God will meet her and win her again. She will renew her vows of loyalty and this time will be true to them; she will take up again the civilization of the sown land and the city, and will not in so doing lose her soul.

God's end in judgement is never therefore the vindication of any abstract principle or any moral order of the universe; it is the final good of persons whom He has made and for whom He continues to care, even when they have ceased to care for Him. Just because His love is so true it cannot let evil go unrebuked; it is by confronting men inescapably with the consequences of their wrong choices that He hopes to persuade them to the right choices next time. But equally, when He is forced thus to pain His children, He does not remain aloof and unmoved. If our human waywardness brings suffering upon earth it introduces sorrow into heaven. 'Forty years long was I grieved with this generation' (Psalm 95^{10}). There is an analogue in God to what in us is disappointment. That comes to expression in the Bible again and again, but perhaps most poignantly in Isaiah's Song of the Vineyard and in Jesus weeping over Jerusalem. Grief includes what wrath does not, the element of love which is surely integral to the divine holiness. And it includes the pain which love must accept when its hope is thwarted. 'Thus saith the Lord: Behold, that which I have built will I break down, and that which I have planted I will pluck up; and this in the whole land' (Jeremiah 45^4). God has called man into being, only to find him reluctant to accept His purpose of good. Hence He must take back what He has given, pull down what men have built wrongly, that He may clear a space for a fresh attempt of love to persuade them to build aright. This is His sentence, His judgement, His doom upon sin, but He brings it in sorrow and not in anger.

VI CONSCIENCE

Let us now consider whither the argument has so far brought us. It is clear that the relation between God and man must be expressed, not in metaphysical terms, but in personal and ethical terms. God is not the absolute

substance of which we are the modes; we are His creatures and His children, bound to Him in loyalty and love.
The concept of creation is of value largely because it
makes possible this kind of ethical relation. In our own
human experience, to bring into being another person
is to be bound thereafter to that person in solicitude; we
feel that there is something wrong and *unnatural* where
the tie between parent and child remains a purely natural
one and is not accompanied by mutual affection. We
cannot say that for God to have called man into being
gives man a claim upon Him; we can say that it confers
upon man a status, gives him a worth in God's eyes which
will never be denied to him. So the fact that God created
Israel as a nation is made by the prophet the ground of
His assurance that that nation will be sustained by Him
in all the vicissitudes of its fortune (Isaiah 43 [1f.]). 'I have
made, and I will bear' (Isaiah 46 [4]). If man emanated
from God's innermost being or were a caprice of His
fantasy it might well not follow that He cared for him.
But that God should create man and then be careless of
his welfare—why, that would make Him not God at all,
but a devil!

If this is so, it follows that the pivot on which the
whole relation between God and man turns is that of the
conscience. Man has a vocation to which he may or may
not rise, as he himself decides. There was a purpose in
the making of him, and it is for him to say whether that
purpose will be fulfilled or frustrated. There is an analogy
here with the call of Israel as the great prophets interpreted it. That did not, as the popular religion supposed,
bind God once for all to this people; it made them His
just in proportion to their response to His will in obedience
and loyalty. The point at which man finds God near to
him or far from him is in his conscience, for God is near
to us as we acknowledge Him and far from us as we turn

from Him to other allegiances. 'The fact is', writes a
Jewish scholar, 'that the nearness of God is determined
by the conduct of man, and by his realization of His
nearness, that is, by his knowledge of God. "Thus taught
the sages, Thy deeds will bring thee near (to God), and
thy deeds will remove thee (from God)."'[16]

This emphasis on the ethical should be sufficient to
mark off the position here maintained from any form of
pantheism. One main error of pantheism is that it con-
ceives the divine presence in the world statically and
spatially, as that of a thing within other things. Here it
is understood dynamically, as an activity which elicits,
sustains, and directs other activities. God is not in the
world as the sap is in the tree not even as the soul is in
the body. He is in it as the father is in the family, as the
leader is in the group He called into being and whose
flagging interest is continually being rekindled at His
enthusiasm. God is the Supreme Self who creates other
selves and endows them with a relative independence
over against Himself. From that point on 'God and man
do not divide the government of the world between them;
man's action is enclosed in God's action, but it is still real
action.'[17]

Perhaps it is along these lines that we can best do
justice to the paradox of Christian faith that God is at
once transcendent and immanent. We can understand
what this means if we think, not of God's relation to the
world, but of His manifestation in and to conscience.
Note the words that one uses at this point: 'in' and 'to'
conscience. The divine holiness is apprehended by us as
something which we can share even while it is infinitely
beyond us. The precept, 'Be ye holy, for I am holy',
presupposes this dual relation. In Elijah's vision, we have

[16] Solomon Schechter: *Some Aspects of Rabbinic Theology* (1909), p. 33.
[17] Martin Buber: op. cit., p. 110.

the sense of having arrived at something inward when we have passed beyond the wind, the earthquake, and the fire, to the still, small voice. Yet he who has heard that voice knows that it subdues his soul by a sublimity and majesty which no forces of nature can possess. The will of God is something to which we aspire, yet it is also something which we can incorporate into our lives here and now. It is so rich that our experience will never exhaust it, yet so simple that we can act on it at this instant. We can borrow the language of C. C. J. Webb and say that 'ultimacy' and 'immediacy' are characteristic of God.[18] It is the God who makes heaven His throne and takes earth as His footstool who says: 'To this man will I look, even to him that is poor and of a contrite spirit, and that trembleth at my word' (Isaiah 66[2]).

Perhaps we can go farther and say that, in a sense, it is for us to determine whether God is near or far, transcendent only or immanent also. There is a saying of the rabbis: 'Before Abraham made God known to His creatures, He was only the God of the heaven; but afterwards He became (through Abraham's proselytizing activity) also the God of the earth.'[19] God, that is to say, enters the world wherever He finds a dedicated soul; where such is lacking, He remains estranged from us, not by His own will, but by ours.

If this is so, then we must restate the whole question of the relation between God and man in more personal and imperative language. I must cease to think of God and man as two terms in a relation which I merely survey and analyse. Am I not myself included under 'man'? Is not the relation therefore one in which I am personally involved? We began by asking whether the human is opposed to the divine or stands at the service of its self-

---

[18] *Religion and Theism* (1934), p. 15.
[19] Quoted in Schechter: op. cit., p. 33.

fulfilment. But there is no such thing as 'the human', there are countless individual men and women, each capable of a personal relation to God. Of these I am one. The question therefore which is brought home to me in my conscience is: Am *I* as an individual opposed to God or do *I* stand at the service of His purpose? Is there so much less of His presence and power in the world, because I have failed Him? We begin with the relation between God and man as a problem for the intellect. But we are not allowed to remain there. It becomes transformed before our eyes, till at last we discover that it is a challenge to the will.

'There is a God; His will is made known to me in Holy Scripture and in conscience. This God wishes to inter-vene in the world. But how is He to do it except with the help of, i.e. *per*, man? Now one can say, we can all say: Yes, that is of course what He does, but not *per* me. No one of us wishes to be that individual; for if God is to intervene in the world it must be through the individual.'[20]

Note. In this discussion nothing has been said of God's relation to nature. Pantheism would assimilate history to nature ('As full, as perfect, in a hair as heart'). The writers of the Bible belong to a pre-scientific age and tend to do the same. God is active in all that happens. He hardens Pharaoh's heart and directs the armies of Cyrus, as He sends or withholds rain in punishment for sin or at the prayer of a prophet. We, however, must distinguish between those activities of God which create and maintain a fixed order of things as the setting for the development of persons and those other activities by which He enters, from moment to moment, into the experience of individuals. Just so the schoolmaster both

[20] Kierkegaard: *Journals* (1938), 1161.

provides a time-table, text-books, a system of discipline, and so on, and deals sympathetically with this or that pupil as his individual difficulties require. There must be an impersonal dealing of God with men if He is to fashion them into persons. For personality is made, not only by response to a love which counts the hairs on our head, but also by the acceptance of a state of things in which the sun rises on just and unjust alike. The practice of morality requires a nature that is indifferent to morality.

Chapter Two

The Cross

I THE GUILTY CONSCIENCE

IT WAS ARGUED in the previous chapter that conscience is the point at which man makes contact with God. By this is meant, of course, not the mere possession of conscience, but its exercise in moral discernment and moral obedience. Here, however, a problem emerges. In the very moment in which we become aware of our capacity for moral discernment, we seem to find that we have already refused moral obedience to some degree. Our earliest insights in this sphere are accompanied by the realization that we are already committed to the wrong cause. Paul describes this in his autobiographical passage in Romans: 'I was alive apart from the law once: but when the commandment came, sin revived, and I died' (7⁹). The state of innocence was disrupted by the instruction which made him aware of his duty. But he did not find himself at that moment in a neutral condition, so that the possibility of guilt lay purely in the future. No! He had already contracted guilt. For, of course, the awakening of conscience is a gradual process and the first steps toward moral maturity, like the later ones, are accompanied by the sense of shame, regret for wrong done, and the weakening of the will which results from commitments already entered upon to our cost.

From now on, therefore, we must think and speak of the guilty conscience. There is as it were a stain upon us, we have contracted guilt. This infidelity to earlier

insights brings with it several perils, not the least of which
is a certain clouding of future insights. The inner voice
may continue for a while its protests against our disobe-
dience, but those protests will grow feebler in course of
time and eventually we may silence the rebuke altogether.
'If therefore the light that is in thee be darkness, how
great is the darkness!' (Matthew 6²³). But we may
content ourselves at this point with an analysis of what
is involved in guilt against a person, where the reproach
of conscience has not yet lost its force. If we reflect on what
we ourselves have gone through, we shall find that under
such circumstances we are in a strait betwixt two. We feel
at one and the same time that an insurmountable barrier
has been built up—and that by our action—between ourselves and the other person, and that we cannot live except
as this barrier is somehow surmounted and the broken
relation between us is restored. It is just this terrible sense
of having lost what we most value, of craving for something which we have ourselves made impossible, that gives
to remorse its haunting quality. The prodigal returning
home longs to be a son again in his father's house. But
that, he sees clearly, can never be; in view of what he has
become by his own folly, he cannot aspire to be more than
a servant. But, at least, as servant he may be able to make
some amends for the wrong he has done and to prove that
he is not the wholly selfish waster that his past would show
him to be. That is his repentance as Jesus describes it in
the parable.

The prodigal resolves in this way to live down the past
and go home. But everything is still uncertain to him till
he actually approaches his home and meets his father
again. Whether he will be received as a servant is something which he cannot decide, it is in his father's hands.
That is to say, when we have sinned against a person, we
know that the final possibility of a restoration of the lost

relationship is with him and not with us. We are thrown on his mercy. That is the meaning of forgiveness, the act of the injured party by which he breaks down the barrier we have set between ourselves and him and makes our meeting possible once more. Where our self-reproach is keenest, where, that is, we feel that the fault is wholly ours, we do not for a moment imagine that we have any claim upon the other. Even our penitence—and how urgent our penitence is!—cannot earn forgiveness. That must be a spontaneous action on the part of the other if it is to be of any avail.

But the very intensity of our longing for forgiveness seems to argue against us that we never can be forgiven. For we do not wish the liberating word to be spoken by the other except in full awareness of what we have done. If we find him disposed to extenuate our guilt or in ignorance as to the true nature of our act, we feel it incumbent on us to insist on their full gravity. Or, if the other person turned out to be morally lax, so that he condoned our wrongdoing as something that really did not matter, we should desist from our appeal to him, since forgiveness on such terms would not be worth having. Only when the words 'I forgive' are spoken by one who is fully informed on what has happened, who knows our worthlessness for exactly what it is, and yet is willing to take us back—only so are they with power. Then the burden of the past falls from our shoulders and we can step out again on the road that runs into the unknown future. But what gives us this assurance, be it noted, is not at all that we have repented, but that the other has forgiven us. Our repentance can never be more than a prayer for his forgiveness.

This description applies fully only to the case in which we are convinced that the fault is, as I said, wholly on our side. That, of course, is a state of things which never actually obtains in human relations. Various degrees of approximation to it are possible, but no more. Human forgiveness is often rightly based in part on the fact that none of us is without guilt, that the wrongdoer has acted to some extent in ignorance, that the injured party is only too well aware that had he been in the other's place he might well have acted as he did. Sometimes we maintain a stubborn attitude toward one who seeks for reconciliation till some turn of events persuades us that we are but human after all and should not let the sun go down upon our wrath. Or we say that we forgive, but do not forget, by which we mean in fact that we are not willing to forgive, that the most we can attain to is not to press our quarrel with the other. We will let the matter drop, but there is to be no genuine reconciliation. In a world of imperfect human beings that kind of evasive dealing with sin has often to be accepted as all that is possible to us. But it cannot satisfy. It does not heal.

Clearly, divine forgiveness is healing because it is of a different quality altogether. It is based on an even clearer perception of my guilt than my most anguished moments of repentance can bring to me. It sets out from a standard of absolute holiness which is beyond my apprehension and the employment of which discredits me altogether. But this very severity in the divine approach to my sin is the guarantee that, if God does forgive, His will be a final dealing with my sin. He is the supreme court of appeal and if, while I am condemned there, I am at the same time received back into fellowship, what is there in the universe that need daunt me henceforth? 'He will tread our iniquities under foot: and thou wilt cast all their sins into the depths of the sea' (Micah 7 [19]). True, conscience may continue to reproach me, but I have an answer to all the arguments it can bring forward out of the past. That answer is that God knows me better even than my conscience does and still does not cast me off. By this we 'shall assure our heart before him [God], whereinsoever our heart condemn us; because God is greater than our heart, and knoweth all things' (1 John 3¹⁹ᶠ·). Omniscience does not act on inadequate knowledge, absolute holiness is not disposed to relax standards, and if these open the door of the prison and bid me go free, how should I fear that some underling will come along and order my re-arrest? The forgiveness of God is a final solution of the problem which the guilty conscience raises, nay, rather, which the guilty conscience *is*.

II   THE MINISTRY OF JESUS

We should be doing less than justice to the Gospel narrative were we to say merely that, for those who accepted Him, Jesus solved this problem of the guilty conscience. We must go behind that, for it seems clear that, in the case of many such persons, it was He who first raised the problem. That is indicated, for example, in the story of Zacchæus. What attracted this man to Jesus in the first instance we do not know; he may simply have been caught up in the popular excitement by which the Master was surrounded. But the first impulse to a new life only came as Jesus took the initiative and offered His friendship. The declaration that he was, in spite of everything, a member of the community, a child of Abraham, went home to him as the ostracism amid which he lived continually could never have done. Had he not been an unworthy member of the community? What could he do to set right the wrongs of which he knew himself to be guilty? So behind the story of the woman who wept out her penitence at the feet of Jesus we can see that somehow He had made her ashamed of what previously she had not questioned. That other woman taken in adultery—was not her most searching experience that which came when all her accusers had left her and she was alone with a strange and challenging purity?

We cannot do justice to the ministry of forgiveness which Jesus exercised till we take into account the awful risk that was at the heart of it. He was accused by His opponents among the Pharisees of sitting loose to plain moral distinctions, of obscuring what was so central and so vital in Old Testament religion, the indissoluble relation between fellowship with God and moral conduct. How could one who spoke in the name of God and passed for a teacher be so lax in His standards? How could He, in defiance of what is so clearly set out in Psalm 1 as the duty of the good man, associate with publicans and sinners? Jesus did, in fact, decline to accept the current classification; it was part of His message that the first would be last and the last first. His mission was not to the righteous, but to sinners. His relations with people were in a sense 'beyond good and evil', that is to say, He did not choose His associates in accordance with their moral congruity. The question remained whether this course of conduct was the outcome of indifference and laxity or was the expression of a holiness so confident of itself that it could mix with evil in an intention of mercy and know that the issue would vindicate it.

The influence of Jesus upon Zacchæus and his like was so potent because it fulfilled the essential conditions of forgiveness. By what He was even more than by what He said, He united an uncompromising judgement upon sin with an unlimited compassion toward the sinner. He rose above the current morality which condemned these people just because He was the spokesman of a higher morality and a far more potent rebuke. Men could harden themselves against the censure of their fellows, they were defenceless against an awe-inspiring purity which found an unexpected ally in their own consciences. When others condemned them, pride could always suggest a retort and a self-justification; when He entered into their lives, though His voice was gentle and His words void of reproach, they could not but condemn themselves. Peter's cry, 'Depart from me; for I am a sinful man, O Lord,' expressed what many others felt. He was a tribunal which they did not dare to face, because the accuser was always a voice within themselves.

When Jesus therefore received these people and spoke to them His word of forgiveness, He brought a liberation which was absolute. Such an assurance on His lips authenticated itself as no one else's condonation or even compassion could have done. Whatever the Pharisee may have thought about it, the publican at whose table Jesus sat did not feel that the guest was compromising Himself by accepting his invitation. The hope which the mere presence of one so gracious brought to him was grounded on the fact that His purity was beyond question. If therefore such a one could receive him and count him still a child of God, what was there in his past or in the contempt of his fellows which could hold him back from a new life? What he had been was something quite different from what he was now, with the companionship of Jesus. Forgiveness did not just deal with the past, it was a guarantee of the future as well. That is implied in the words which Jesus used more than once: 'Go, and sin no more.' Life need never again be what it had been, for wherever a man went he carried with him the glad knowledge that precisely where there was an unquestionable purity he had found an unquestioning love. True, questions had been asked, questions which he had never expected to have put to him, but they had been forced upon him by his own conscience. In the very moment at which his sin was forgiven, it became so hateful in his eyes that he disowned it, cast it out of himself for ever.

All this was possible because the dimension, as it were,

in which the forgiveness of Jesus moved was divine rather than human. I do not mean by that simply that, as is related in the story in Mark 2, Jesus spoke words which seemed blasphemous to those for whom it was axiomatic that forgiveness was the prerogative of God. In that incident Jesus claims to act as God's representative on earth, as one who is for the time being invested with His authority. I mean rather that the peace of conscience which Jesus brought to those who accepted His Gospel was final, not subject to the limitations and doubts which qualify any forgiveness such as we extend to one another. He spoke as one who gave a sentence from which there could be no appeal and it was received as such. That is presupposed in all the piety of the early Church. It is quite true that 'no early Christians ever thought of Jesus as really their God, whatever were their glowing tributes of prayer and praise to Him'.[1] Still, they did turn to Him for what only God could give, and found that their prayers were answered. We may postpone any attempt to explain this, it is enough to stress again here that there was that in the forgiveness of Jesus which left men persuaded that the sentence of emancipation He had uttered would not be called in question for a moment, even were the case transferred to the tribunal of God Himself.

III THE CROSS

So far, we have considered only what happened during the life and ministry of Jesus. We must now go on to translate what has been said of the past into the language of the present. It is the testimony of Christian experience through the ages, from Saul on the Damascus road and Augustine with the words *Tolle, lege; tolle, lege* ringing in his ears, to the men and women of missionary

[1] J. Moffatt: *1 Corinthians* (1938) in the *Moffatt Commentary*, p. 251.

lands in our own day, that He who spoke forgiveness long ago in Galilee continues to speak it still. Stories like those of the penitent woman and Zacchæus the publican win the hearts of individuals who feel that their condition is mirrored in them and that therefore the assurance of release is for them also. The words, 'Neither do I condemn thee, go and sin no more', are heard now as spoken to them personally. And their efficacy is precisely what it was when those words were first uttered; that is, they convince the hearer that the divine holiness before which they stand rebuked is yet with them in mercy.

But, of course, it is not merely these stories which mediate to us in after generations such forgiveness as only God can offer. They are reinforced by what has happened since the events which they relate, by the Cross and Resurrection, and by the presence of Christ in the Christian fellowship through which we have access to these. For the Cross is the most prominent of a whole class of events, whose characteristic it is to belong to the present, though they are dated in the past. It is a commonplace nowadays that there are two kinds of time: the one, time that is registered on the calendar and the other, time that is actually lived through. If we work with the second, we can define the present as that complex of events which enters formatively at any moment into the making of my selfhood; the past will then include everything which has spent its force. The present is part of me, the past is the baggage I carry, as it were. Thus what is present for one man can be past for another, or what was past for me yesterday can become present for me today. An illustration will show what is meant. An incident of some years ago left its mark upon me at the time, but it has long since been forgotten; a visit to a certain place or an encounter with a certain person reinstates that incident, I burn with resentment or am consumed with regret. The past has become present again for me.

The Cross of Christ possesses to the highest degree the potentiality of such movement from the past to the present. When it lays hold upon us, when we turn to it with receptive hearts, it communicates to us the divine holiness in judgement and the divine mercy in forgiveness as nothing else can do. Let us consider how it does this.

The Cross of Christ is the severest judgement that can be passed upon sin, it exposes it without reserve. It does this for the actors in the tragedy of Calvary. The death of Jesus has preserved for ever in the memory of the race those who took part in it. They imagined themselves to be participating merely in something that would be soon over and as soon forgotten; but every one of them has become fixed in history for all time. Never shall we forget the disciple who turned against his Master and sold Him to His enemies; his treachery becomes proverbial, so that even at the height of its anti-God propaganda Soviet Russia brands as Judases those who question the régime. What of Pilate, the man who sinned against his conscience that he might keep his office, only to forfeit both in the end? Or the ecclesiastical politician Caiaphas—a solemn warning of the hideous wrongs of which men become guilty once they use expediency as their criterion? Or those others, the disciples who slipped away and left Jesus to His fate while they made themselves safe, the soldiers who just did the day's inhuman work and then worked off their boredom with the dice? These are human types, caught in their characteristic attitudes as men are in no-man's-land when the flare goes up.

But much the same may be said of every generation since them. The Cross moves through the centuries and as it goes it exposes the evasion, the cowardice, and the self-centredness of men as nothing else does. If we today are in any respect more sensitive than our fathers, if conscience is more quick to discern the fine shades of good or to pierce through the disguises which evil assumes, our education has largely come from the Cross. Those who are accustomed to enter into Holy Week with any awareness of what happened long ago in Jerusalem as of significance for all men and all ages, know how they are searched and probed at such a time. A Good Friday service can lay bare one's very soul, so that the kind of thing one has accepted the year through as inevitable or even as justified now becomes a burning shame. How could I be so petty, so clamorous for my own rights and so neglectful of another's needs, in a world in which that life was poured out without reserve for the unthankful and the undeserving? The most scathing judgement I can pass on myself in such a mood of self-examination is that I have a part, today, in the crucifixion of the Lord.

But, accompanying this, there is the sense that somehow the Cross was meant for me. 'The Son of God, who loved me, and gave himself up for me' (Galatians 2²⁰). That is not an historical judgement, I do not assert that my existence and need were present to the consciousness of Jesus as He breathed His last. It is an apprehension of how exactly He meets my situation, as when one lays down a book and says: 'That was written for me.' The Cross sets out and solves the problems I wrestle with, gives voice to my most secret aspirations, knows me better than I know myself. The Cross does not broadcast some general offer of forgiveness, it so speaks home to my conscience that I feel that precisely *my* sin is under the judgement of God most holy, yet does not thrust me out from God most merciful. There is a tale of a monastery in which there was a picture of the Divine Face such that, wherever one stood to look at it, it seemed that God's eye was resting upon oneself and singling one out from all the world. There was that individualizing genius in the ministry of Jesus, and the Cross has the same quality as it moves down the centuries. The multitudinous perversities of the human heart are revealed, judged, and overcome by the manifold grace of God.

For the Cross will not accept any estimate of it as merely a noble act of human self-sacrifice; it is borne in upon us that here we reckon with ultimate reality, with the living God Himself. That the self-giving we see there is that of a man like ourselves is clear enough, but this is the vehicle, the expression, the means, of self-giving on the part of God Himself. That is not an inference to be drawn from some Christological doctrine arrived at apart from the Cross; it is itself the starting-point of Christological thinking. The Cross is invested with the numinous, the sacred, that which evokes reverence, awe, and limitless gratitude. The divine reality is self-authenticating, and it is here. He who hears the word of forgiveness and renewal spoken to him from Calvary does not go away and inquire whether what has been said on earth will or will not be confirmed in heaven. Conscience responds to that declaration as it can only respond to a personal utterance on the part of God. At the Cross the shattering of our pride and the uplifting of our penitence are done with a majesty and a certainty which are the marks of God Himself in action. And we go away from the encounter as those who can never be called upon to face some other tribunal. No man can unsay what was said there: 'Go in peace and sin no more.'

IV   THE CROSS IN TIME

We have now to ask what it is in the Cross which gives it such efficacy, how it is that this event in time, a man dying at the hands of His enemies, can become charged with a significance which is eternal. To answer that question, we must attempt first to discover what was in the mind of Jesus as He went to His death, what He Himself understood it to mean.

The sayings anticipatory of death in the Synoptics are few in number and are exposed to doubt. Do they reflect the mind of Jesus or do they read back into His life the faith of the Primitive Church? We must, I think, set aside the clearest reference of all, that in which Jesus declares that He gives Himself 'a ransom for many' (Mark 10[45]). The Lucan parallel is worded differently, so that while the thought of His death as self-sacrifice may well go back to the Master, the explanation of it as a ransom is probably not from Him. Nor can we be confident that the words spoken at the Last Supper have been preserved exactly as they were uttered. In view of the central place which the Supper came to occupy in the life of the Church, it is quite likely that, while the actions of the Lord were faithfully reproduced, something of the Church's confession and thanksgiving came to be incorporated in the words used. If we are to be sure of our ground, therefore, we must confine ourselves to the simple actions of breaking bread and pouring wine, and in each case of distributing it also.

Here I must compress into a paragraph what calls for much fuller treatment. Attention should probably be fixed on the act of breaking rather than on the bread broken, and this in turn interpreted in the light of the acted parables of Old Testament prophecy, such an action being not merely one which foreshadows the future, but one also which serves to bring it about. Jesus broke the bread as the symbol, the pledge, and the beginning of that self-giving which was to take him whithersoever God would have Him to go, even to the Cross, should that be His will. He offers Himself in His self-sacrifice at once to the Father and to those who sit at the table. It is for their sakes, it is the act through which the Kingdom is to come, and in that Kingdom they will have a share. But we must say more than that. In view of what is said elsewhere in the Gospels of the disciple as called to identify himself with the Master even to the bearing of His Cross, Professor T. W. Manson is surely right when he suggests that Jesus hoped that His disciples would go to Calvary with Him.[2] The offering of the broken bread was an invitation to share in what He was about to do. The disciples were not to be passive recipients of His benefits, they were to be active partners in His work.

But how did Jesus conceive that His death would avail for His followers? Here we are left almost entirely to conjecture. There is abundant evidence in the Gospels that He foresaw the coming conflict between His people and Rome and dreaded the suffering and ruin which would be its inevitable outcome. The tears shed over Jerusalem express the sorrow of one who has striven to avert such a doom but fears that His appeal has gone unheeded. The parable of the Barren Fig-tree is spoken by one who regards His ministry as the last opportunity before the nation. When the attention of Jesus was called to events which had raised for His contemporaries the problem of undeserved suffering, He bade His hearers turn their minds to the peril which threatened them all alike (Luke 13^{1-5}). We have at least one awful premonition of the siege and its accompanying horrors (Luke 19^{41-4}).

Now, there is a common human impulse, when one sees a fate of this kind impending over those whom one loves, to offer oneself to do and suffer simply anything, if only thereby they may be spared. There were some noticeable instances of this in the Old Testament, particularly that moving story of Moses on the sacred mountain, when the insane revelry around the golden calf had scarcely died out in the valley below. 'Oh, this people have sinned a great sin, and have made them gods of gold. Yet now, if

[2] *Teaching of Jesus* (1935), pp. 231f.

thou wilt forgive their sin—; and if not, blot me, I pray thee, out of thy book which thou hast written' (Exodus 32 [31 f.]). One must not ask precisely how Moses supposed his life could make atonement for the sin of the people. He had no theory, he was possessed by a love for them which would not permit him to see their ruin and still live. Something of this was in the heart of Paul, when he was prepared even to forfeit his own share in Christ if thereby Israel might be saved (Romans 9 [3]). Was it in some such way as this that Jesus looked forward to the fate in store for His people and, agonizing over them in love, offered Himself to death, in the hope that thereby somehow it might yet be averted? If so, He went to Calvary, not to carry out His part in some scheme of atonement, but at the bidding of a love which could accept anything, however terrible and painful, for itself rather than remain inactive while others suffered. If He could not avert their doom, He could at least share it with them.

That ideas of this kind were current in contemporary Judaism we know. It was one of the means by which the suffering of the faithful under Antiochus Epiphanes was accounted for. When the youngest of the seven brothers goes to martyrdom he does it with the words: 'I, as my brethren, give up both soul and body for the laws of our fathers, calling upon God that he may speedily become gracious to the nation.' There is a propitiatory quality about his sacrifice, it is designed to 'stay the wrath of the Almighty' (2 Maccabees 7 [37 f.]). Still more explicit are the references in a later work: 'Make my blood their purification, and take my life to ransom their lives'; 'Through them our country was purified, they having as it were become a ransom for the nation's sin' (4 Maccabees 6 [29], 17 [20-2]). Here we have a thought-form which stood at the disposal of Jesus, though we need not suppose that there was with Him any idea of 'staying the wrath of the

Almighty'. He accepted His death as a martyr and
offered His life as a prayer that what He dreaded so much
for His people might yet be spared them.

Something of this kind, it may be, is what the death of
Jesus meant to Himself. We have now to ask what it
means to us.

V   THE CROSS IN ETERNITY

We have been working throughout with a dynamic view
of the relation between God and man. For this, there
are no events of a purely human order which have
somehow to be brought into connexion with God. He is
always active in our world, so that what men do from
moment to moment is taken up by Him and wrought into
the pattern of His eternal purpose. The prophetic vision
sees how every event has two sides, one the action of men
and the other that of God. This is so, even when men are
wholly blind to the existence of anything beyond their own
wills: Cyrus the conqueror does not know that, as he
storms a fortress or rifles a palace, he serves the redemp-
tive intention of the mighty God. But it is particularly so
when men are aware of the divine leading and, like the
Suffering Servant, yield themselves to an end beyond their
brief lives. This is especially so with the Cross. Calvary has
a human side to it in the treachery and cowardice which
surrounded it and in the heroic patience with which it was
endured. But what is the deed of God which we are
enabled to discern in it?

It is a deed of holy love, we say. But what exactly does
holy love do? The answer is that love identifies itself with
those for whom it cares, and identifies itself with them
without reserve. It makes their lot its own, refusing any
privilege which would separate it from them, bearing any
hardship which they are constrained to bear. Love

commits one to full participation in the other's lot, as when Moses asked to share his people's doom, if they were not to be forgiven. You measure the extent to which one person cares for another by his readiness to identify himself with him. Think, for example, of the girl in the film *The Best Years of their Lives* who cares so much for the lad who has lost his hands in the war that she does not shrink from the exposure of his injuries, but counts it a privilege to share his disabilities at the point where they are most carefully screened from all other eyes. Or think of the story of Madeleine Barot, the French girl who volunteered during the war to enter as an internee a refugee camp in the Pyrenees, to share its hunger and filth, even going the length of teaching the inmates how to catch and cook rats to supplement their scanty ration. There can be no doubt of a love which is willing to sit where others sit, and to suffer what others suffer, yes, to offer itself to do so.

The Cross then stands for the divine self-identification with humanity. This is the story of an infinite divine condescension which has moved hearts ever since it was first told. It is in our Christmas hymns:

> *He came down to earth from heaven,*
> *Who is God and Lord of all,*
> *And His manger was a stable,*
> *And His cradle was a stall.*

We took that literally once, we thought of a divine being stepping down from His throne above the skies, putting on a robe of human flesh and descending to earth to be born as a man.We know now that such language is poetical, an effort of the devout imagination to present the truth by picture and symbol. What is important is that we should not for all that lose the wonder, the sense of indebtedness, the glad response in devotion, which the Christmas poem has evoked down the ages. What has come to us in Christ is

D

not merely the knowledge that the God who made the world
and holds it in His hands does not keep His dignity, but
abandons it—for us; does not live in isolation, but lives—
with us; does not abide in a painless bliss, but finds His bliss
in the midst of human pain where He can share it with us.
No! what has come to us in Christ is God Himself doing this.

So far, however, we have spoken only of how love
identifies itself with need. But what of sin, the sin, it may
be, of the refusal of love itself? There love takes upon
itself the consequences of another's sin, that by so doing it
may redeem him from that sin in the only effectual way in
which this can be done, by winning him to repudiate it for
ever. Precisely because we are responsible for the confusion into which our deeds have brought the world, love
accepts responsibility for the situation we have created and
seeks by all means in its power to transform it for our good.
Karl Jaspers in his discussion of German war-guilt describes how even one who opposed the Nazi régime may
yet feel that, just because he is a German and the German
land and tongue and people are his inalienably, he must
burn with shame for what was done by evil men in the
name of these and seek to make some atonement for their
crimes.[3] There is, he rightly argues, no such thing as a
collective guilt in which the individual is involved merely
by his membership in a society. But there is a solidarity
of love by which we make the guilt of others our own that
we may free them from it with ourselves.

Does this seem sadly lacking in the precision of the
traditional doctrines of the atonement, with their talk of
a satisfaction rendered to the justice of God, an appease-
ment of His wrath, or a vindication of His injured honour?
That is because legal proceedings and commercial transactions are necessarily more clear-cut than the efforts, appeals, and sacrifices of unselfish love. But we can scarcely

[3] *Die Schuldfrage* (1946), pp. 56ff.

doubt in which direction we are to look for a picture of
what is in the heart of God. It is awe-inspiring to reflect,
for example, that on the Christian view self-effacement is
among the attributes of God. The rabbis had a saying that
in all places where Scripture speaks of the greatness of
God, there it speaks also of His humility. The humility of
the eternal God! How can we ever dissect and rationalize
that? The only adequate appreciation of it is to allow
ourselves to be swept off our feet by it.

God in His love is with us and for us, but He is not
instead of us. He does not, that is to say, take on Himself
our human lot that He may relieve us of it; He does it
that we may be able to accept it with a new spirit and find
in it a way back to His fellowship. His hope is that by
entering into our confusion, tragedy, and pain, He may
lead us out of it, back to His light and holiness and truth.

There is a bold saying in the Greek fathers which, as it
stands, is unacceptable, yet which can be so read as to
yield just the truth I am trying now to set forth. 'He
became man for us that we might become God in Him.'
Karl Barth in his discussion of election has grasped at what
lies behind that formula. It is the gracious will of God so
to bind Himself to men that their utter need becomes His,
and His glory—the glory of love and holiness—becomes
theirs in return. [4]

> *Love seeketh not itself to please,*
> *Nor for itself hath any care,*
> *But for another gives its ease,*
> *And builds a heaven in hell's despair.*

Is there one of us who has not been blessed at some time
with the knowledge of a love which has done as much as
that for him? Just that, on the scale of all time and all
humanity, God Himself has done.

[4] *Kirchliche Dogmatik*, II, 22, §§ 32–5.

VI   THE CROSS IN TIME AND ETERNITY

What we have been saying in this last section may be summed up thus: The Cross is not a contrivance which makes possible, by some nice balance of interests and demands, the unity of holiness and mercy in God. It is the event in time by which this unity is supremely expressed as that which is the very nature of the eternal God. Only an absolutely holy love could identify itself with the fallen and the sinful while itself remaining unstained thereby. Only such a love could vindicate its own purity by their redemption, never entertaining the thought that it might do so by their punishment. God is at once the moral order of the universe and the love that cares for the individual soul, and nowhere does He show Himself more evidently such than when He accepts as His own what that soul suffers by its violation of the moral order. As long as we suppose that God first does or receives something on the basis of which He then subsequently forgives, we do not understand what forgiveness is with God. We still err by robbing it of its sweep and majesty, making it something as petty as our own. As we have seen, it is the nature of God's forgiveness that, in the act of receiving home those who have sinned against Him, He establishes His righteousness more surely than ever before, and that in the only place that matters, the conscience.

But the Cross is not just the demonstration that God is prepared to forgive, it is God Himself in the act of forgiving. 'God was in Christ, reconciling the world unto himself, not reckoning unto them their trespasses' (2 Corinthians 5[19]). We must get away from the notion of a remote God who does something in heaven or somewhere like that far away and who then has to solve the problem of how to get to us what He has done. God acts in time and space, He is involved deeply in our human affairs. The patience with which He endures our perversity, generation by generation, is the patience of a God who is too holy to allow other than bitter fruits to grow on the tree of sin and also too loving to leave us to that bitterness without hope. His presence with us *is* His forgiveness, His continual acceptance of our lot *is* the hope that He may lead us through it back to Himself. God does not have His special seasons in which He is prepared to forgive, His whole dealing with us is a marvel of forgiveness. It is such even when we shut our hearts to His appeal and render His forgiveness null and void. For then too God waits to be gracious, since it is His property to forgive without limit. We need to recover the early Christian sense of a great and saving deed of God which was done once and abides for ever. God in Christ *has* forgiven. Whether He will do so or not is not an open question. Whether we will respond in our hearts to that forgiveness or shut against it—ah! that *is* an open question.

But the language we have used in this last paragraph seems to imply that we have shifted our ground somewhat. We have passed from the Cross as an event in past time to the forgiving patience of God by which we live in the present. That raises at once the question of the relation between the cross on Calvary and the Cross which is for ever in the heart of God. I have by implication rejected the suggestion that the divine forgiveness is attached simply and solely to the death of Jesus nineteen hundred years ago. That could only be maintained by harking back to a view which we have found highly unsatisfactory; the view, I mean, that there was some sort of transaction then on the basis of which forgiveness became possible to God. Yet, while we do not tie the mercy of God to one occasion in the past, we shall not go so far in the other direction as to make that occasion a mere symbol of a general principle that God forgives, that in Him there is no holiness that is not also mercy and no mercy that is not also holiness.

We have to consider the relation between the mercy of God in which we live and move and have our being and the mercy of God which reaches us in Christ. Perhaps language will help us here. The substantive 'cross' yields the adjective 'crucial'. A crucial turn of events is one which is decisive, which settles once for all whether things are thus or thus. The Cross is of this order. How it is so we shall see more fully when we have discussed the Christological question which comes next. But something we can say now. If there was one of our race in whom God Himself came to us in a peculiar sense, if in Him the very holy love of God took flesh and walked among us, and if His fate was to be rejected and slain, then we look on with awe and trembling to see what the issue will be for God and man. If, in the face of this and by means of this, God's holy love enters afresh into the world, more gloriously clear and more splendidly convincing than ever before, then we can be sure that there is nowhere where it is not present, that we do not draw breath otherwise than in God's mercy. What was in the Cross was so decisive, so *crucial*, that it must be everywhere.

But this, of course, is not an argument. It is an insight, a discernment. As such it is possible only to one who has been humbled and yet uplifted by the Cross, whose whole being has been claimed by it as a deed of God for him personally, a deed of that holiness which is also mercy. Salvation does not follow on that experience. That experience is itself salvation. For no one can pass through it and remain the same. He must be reborn in liberation from the past, in heartfelt gratitude and lifelong devotion.

Chapter Three

Christil

I DIVINE AND HUMAN

THE CHRISTOLOGICAL formula, 'Two natures in one person', is not a solution of the Christological problem. It is a statement of it. The whole argument of the last chapter has gone to show that in Jesus Christ we have to do with a life which is at once genuinely human, as human as our own, and fraught with the judgement and mercy of God. If He were less unreservedly one with us, we should doubt His will to help us. Were He less assuredly exalted above us in our need, it would be His competence that would be called in question. Again, Christian devotion cannot afford to dispense either with the simple following of the man Jesus, as we see it in Francis of Assisi, or with the awed gratitude which recognizes in the Cross the very self-giving of the Godhead. We have therefore in His life just that co-operation between divine and human elements which we have seen to penetrate all our experience, but in a special form. For it is this divine-human reality which, in New Testament language, reconciles man to God, or, in the language we are employing here, transfers us from a relation in which God and man are opposed to one in which they are in harmony.

The difficulty is to find categories in which to express this divine-human fact with which we have to do. The traditional categories are inadequate for a number of reasons. In the first place, they derive from a psychology and a metaphysic which are no longer intelligible to us.

Neither 'nature' nor 'person' means in the creeds what we
mean by the words today. In the second place, while no
doubt it was the concern of those responsible for them to
do justice both to the divinity and to the humanity in
Christ, what they actually did was to sacrifice the latter
to the former. Before we censure them for that, we should
at least make some allowance for the fact that the Fourth
Gospel had set such a tendency in operation already. One
has only to compare John's account of the Agony with that
of Mark to see that this is so. On how faithfully he was
followed, a modern theologian may be quoted. Dr H. R.
Mackintosh tells us, writing of the traditional Christology,
that 'its persistent obscuration of Jesus' real manhood
proves that after all it shrank from the thought of a true
"kinsman Redeemer"—one of ourselves in flesh and
spirit. Christ's point of departure was Godhead, yet in
His descent He stopped half-way. The quasi-manhood
He wore is so filled with divine powers as to cease to belong
to the human order.'[1]

At this point we have to face the other possibility, the
one forced upon us by the critical and historical study of
Christian origins. Is it possible that the human in Jesus
Christ is all there ever was, that the divine is simply the
reading back into His life of the devotion and gratitude of
His followers? Or, to go even farther than that, was the
historical Jesus the merest lay-figure upon whom the early
Christians, Paul in particular, hung the ideas they derived
from Jewish apocalyptic or the mystery-religions? My
reply to such a suggestion would be that historical study
does not dissipate the mystery of Christ in this way, but
rather carries it back to the very beginning. I do not see
how it is possible to recover any historical figure from the
Gospels other than one who is governed by a profound
sense of mission, who feels Himself to be acting for God in

[1] *The Doctrine of the Person of Jesus Christ* (1913), p. 467.

the world and to be bringing His time to a crisis of decision, one, again, who breaks with the conventional classification of people as 'righteous' and 'sinners' and by a sovereign act of mercy opens the kingdom of God to the outcasts of His day.

I do not doubt, therefore, that in essentials faith derives from Christ and not Christ from faith. We are now in a position to begin our search for new categories.

(a) It is in accordance with all that has been said so far if at this point we insist that Christology must work with dynamic, not static, categories. As Karl Barth says in the latest volume of his *Dogmatik*, man does not have a history, he *is* one. Human nature is not a mysterious something which stands behind our acts, it expresses itself in those acts and is only known in and through such self-expression.[2] So it must be with Christ, and Barth is clear on that point also.[3] We need to break down the distinction between His person and His work, for the one cannot be discussed, cannot even be visualized, apart from the other. We are not to look for God in some nature which He brought ready-made into the world, but in the whole sweep of His life from birth to death and beyond that to victory over death. 'God was in Christ' means that He was in Him in all that he underwent, all that He did and suffered, in all the experiences of a personality that developed as ours does.

(b) We must discard metaphysical categories in favour of ethical ones. We belong to the post-Kantian period in philosophy for which, where the question of God is concerned, the centre of interest has once for all been shifted from the cosmos to conscience. God is to be found by obedience to the inner voice rather than by observation of

[2] Of course, it is not exhausted in those acts. Through what a man *does*, we may glimpse something far richer which he *is*.
[3] *Kirchliche Dogmatik*, III, 2, § 44.

nature. That 'moralization of doctrine' for which P. T.
Forsyth so often called needs to be carried much farther,
certainly farther than he himself was prepared to take it.
Yet we are still apt to think that if the divine love is incarnate in Jesus Christ that is something less than if a
divine substance were lodged in Him. But, if there is any
truth in the biblical view of things, ultimate reality is a
personal God and His dealing with men, so that if we are
able to express Christ in terms drawn from ethical and
personal relationships, we are moving in a region higher
than that of metaphysics. Or should we perhaps say that
we have reached the true metaphysic? Let me again quote
Dr Mackintosh on this point: 'If we are inspired by
Christian faith to affirm that Jesus Christ is identical with
God in will—a will manifested in His achievement, we
have reached a point beyond which no advance is possible.
. . . In every conceivable sense in which this is a *true*
estimate of His person, it also is a metaphysical estimate.'[4]

(*c*) This second point calls for further elaboration.
Between our doctrine of Christ's person and our conception
of salvation there must be an intimate connexion, just
because He is our Saviour. In Athanasius a metaphysical
conception of salvation led necessarily to a Christology of
the metaphysical order. He was able to accept in the end
the term *homoousios* which he had originally avoided
because it was in fact required by the principles from which
he set out. If salvation is by the transmutation of corrupt
human nature into incorruptible divine nature, if it is a

---

[4] op. cit., p. 304. So Aulén: 'If God is "spirit," then there is nothing
more "substantial" and *essential* than His will and disposition of heart. If
we should speak of a substantial unity which would mean something other
than this unity of disposition, we would thereby assert something less rather
more.' *The Faith of the Christian Church* (1948), pp. 213f. So Knox: 'Christ
is of one substance with the Father; but the utmost, and inmost it is given
us to know of God's "substance" is that He is love—as such He is revealed
in Christ—and love is not a metaphysical essence, but personal moral will
and action.' *On the Meaning of Christ* (1947) p. 57.

change of substance, then we must be sure that he who comes to save us is of one substance with the Father. But, our idea of salvation being changed, there is of necessity a change in our Christology. If we are brought out of sin into holiness, then what we need to be assured of is that Christ is competent to pronounce God's judgement on our sin and to remake us by the power of God's holiness. For that He must be one in will with the Father. Whether He is also one in substance is immaterial. For clearly two persons may be of the same substance yet different in their purposes. Thus we see here again that the ethical categories are higher than the metaphysical or, if one prefers to put it so, they are the truly metaphysical ones.

(d) The unit of history—and that is what we are seeking—is not an individual person, it is a situation. Such a situation is ordered around any one of a number of centres, each centre being constituted by a single person. Thus the world-situation is one thing today in its bearing upon the Prime Minister and another in its bearing on myself. And it is the message of the Bible that each situation can be seen from two points of view, it has an upper level and a lower one. At the lower level it is a piece of secular history, Cyrus marching on Babylon, for example. At the upper level it is part of the working-out in time of the eternal divine purpose, a stage—to take the illustration just used —in the deliverance of mankind from superstition and fear. The language so often used nowadays of a divine 'irruption into history' presupposes a God-less view of history. History is first surrendered wholly to human purposes and then God is brought in by some violent means. But history, we have urged, is not apart from God, it is the drama of divine-human interaction. That is true of all situations, true pre-eminently of the situation with which we are here concerned, that which was constituted around Jesus as centre, the sum-total of His experiences.

As we shall see later, that situation extends far beyond His earthly life and death, but for the time being we can do best by keeping within these limits. The formula I propose is therefore 'two aspects in one situation' in place of 'two natures in one person'. Those two aspects are the divine and the human. What is at one level the life and adverse fortunes of a Jewish carpenter in the first century of our era is at another level the crowning deed of God in time.

In so far as such an approach can claim the sanction of any of the traditional Christologies, it will look to the East and not to the West. In one of the latest expositions of Orthodox thought stress is laid on the 'theandric' quality of God's activity in Christ, and we are told that 'the incarnation involves intimate co-inherence, interchange and mutual appropriation of the human and the divine'.[5] The language is akin to that which we have already employed, with of course the considerable difference that we see this 'interchange and mutual appropriation', not as between two elements in a person, but as between two partners in a developing situation.[6]

II TWO MOVEMENTS

There is a striking passage in Forsyth which elaborates just such a suggestion as is here made. 'God and man meet in humanity, not as two entities or natures which coexist, but as two movements in mutual interplay, mutual struggle, and reciprocal communion. On the one hand we have an initiative, creative, productive action, clear and sure, on the part of eternal and absolute God; on the other hand we have the seeking, receptive, appropriating action of groping, erring, growing man. . . . We have these

---

[5] F. Lampert: *The Apocalypse of History* (1948), p. 123.
[6] That is, the position here taken up is Nestorian and Antiochene, not Alexandrian.

two movements permeating the whole life of historic humanity, and founding its spiritual psychology. . . . All spiritual history is action. History is action, and reciprocal action. It is commerce, and even conflict, with the transcendent. . . . If the whole drama of the soul of man could be compressed into one narrow neck and one strait gate, that is what we should have—the tremendous friction (so to say) of these two currents within a personal experience.'[7] My contention in what follows is, quite simply, that 'the whole drama of the soul of man' is so compressed in Jesus Christ, and that its 'tremendous friction' culminates in the Cross.[8]

Let us however take time to analyse further what the interlocking of these two movements involves. We may select as our analogy the relation between a scientific research worker and the student who has come to him for training. What the scientist is concerned to communicate is not his knowledge, but his skill, he wants the student to develop that uncanny insight, that flair for the essential which are characteristic of the master. So he discloses to him without reserve the procedures which he adopts and hopes that the student will follow him and grow, while retaining his independence, into the likeness of his master. And the other, on his side, does not feel that he is being reduced to dependence on the master; he feels rather that each new phase in the assimilation of what he offers enlarges his powers and his capacity to do independent work. So in God's activity in the world, He has no end in view for which He seeks to utilize persons, His end is the making of those persons themselves. He wishes to

[7] *The Person and Place of Jesus Christ* (1909), pp. 336f.
[8] 'The basic and original phenomenon of religious life is the meeting and mutual interaction between God and man, the movement of God toward man and of man toward God' (Berdyaev: *Freedom and the Spirit* (1935), p. 189). Cf Knox: 'We have tried to interpret the revelation in Christ as a static thing in a person when it was really a dynamic thing taking place in an event' (op. cit., 44).

share with them His own eternal life, for nothing less than that is implied when John tells us that 'as the Father hath life in himself, even so gave he to the Son also to have life in himself' (5^{26}), and that the Son in turn bestows this life on men (4^{14}).

We must think of God therefore as for ever active to bring humanity to Himself, into unity of mind and heart and will with Him. To do this, He is for ever seeking to enter into our human situation as it is, to involve Himself with our humanity in its need and suffering. For He hopes thereby to fashion out of it a family of persons, each of whom is bound to Him and also to his fellows in love. He wishes to bring individuals into a filial relation to Himself, but that carries with it that they recognize one another as brothers in Him. God's love for man aims at awakening him to love for his fellow-man. And in a world tragically astray as ours is, love must express itself in identification with one's fellows to the extent of self-abandonment and the sharing of their lot to the uttermost. So that the family of persons God desires to make will be one of mutual service and sacrifice, in which each will find his own good in the common weal. But the realization of this purpose is not solely God's affair. Since man is free, even God's love can only enter man's world with his consent. Without that consent, the divine concern for mankind and the divine yearning to win it back will remain indeed unchanged, but they will be robbed of their effect. They can only become active in our world as they win the co-operation of human wills.

On the other hand, with the burden of the world upon him and the agony of it in his soul, man seeks after a God who will set all right. His prayers and complaints, his outraged sense of justice and his longing for a fairer order of things, are so many evidences of his search. If he pits himself against his brother for selfish ends, there are times when he will fling his life away as a common thing for that brother's sake. If he is Absalom in revolt against his father, he is also David longing that he might die, and Absalom, the traitor, live. Where in the uncertainty of life is God's will to be found? What is it that He intends with human beings? These are some of the questions he asks. And he has no answer to them. The answer can be given only from beyond, from the side of God. There have been those among us to whom an answer has come. They are the prophetic spirits. And how did the answer come to them? Not, as we shall see, primarily by ecstasy or any abnormal state of consciousness, but by waiting, obedience, prayer, and the dedication of the total self to the will of God in such measure as it was made known. God was seeking a man through whom to act in the world, a man was seeking a God for whom he could act—and the two met!

What happens when these two meet? That entry of God into the world of which we spoke a moment ago now becomes gloriously possible. The divine compassion which overarches us can become a force at work in our midst. It is not that God has a purpose of love and commissions a man to carry it out for Him; that would mean that He Himself does not act, He merely instructs His delegate. Then what we should have would be but that man's suffering love and not God's own. But if, as has been urged, every situation has two sides to it, one invisible and of God, one visible and of man, then something more than this takes place. The divine self-giving is as real an element in the situation we are trying to describe as ever the human is. God actually comes among us as one who is afflicted in our afflictions and suffers at our hands that He may save us from ourselves. But observe, God only enters into the world in such measure as His will to do so is accepted—I say accepted, not necessarily understood—by the man in question. We need not doubt that something of the divine compassion found expression through Jeremiah's heart broken for his people. But was it not also to some extent frustrated by his bitterness against his enemies? Again, God's action is conditioned by man's freedom though His nature is not. There is that which He would fain do, but cannot, since He has not found one sufficiently *en rapport* with Himself. The word remains unspoken, the deed not done.

But suppose God were to find a human life offered to Him in unreserved dedication, placed altogether at His disposal, so that whatsoever He willed to accomplish in the world could be done through it. Would not there be such a meeting then between God and man, such a confluence of these two movements that God would come among us in such a way as He had hoped, since the world began, to be able to come? As such a life reached its maximum in dedication, so would God reach His maximum in liberating and redeeming action among men. The love of such a person for his fellows would be the visible aspect whereof the invisible aspect would be God Himself, holding nothing back but giving Himself in all His grace and truth and power to those who had rejected these things but who still could not live without them, because they were made for them at the first.

Just this is what we see in Jesus Christ.

III　THE MEANING OF THE CROSS

The life of Jesus, it is clear, was lived within certain definite historical limitations. It was a mission to Israel and, whatever the ultimate vista which opened out before the eye of His mind, His ministry was, except for one or two instances, confined to His own people. That does not detract from its greatness, however, since restriction of this kind, concentration on an immediate task, is of the essence of greatness. The master shows himself, not by fretting against the restrictions life imposes on him, but by his use of them. What is done faithfully under one set of circumstances has significance for all circumstances. The wisdom of Plato has something to offer to all subsequent generations, just because it was so apposite to the generation in which it was first given expression. If therefore in what follows we speak of what Jesus did for men rather than what He did for Israel, that is because we looked in the previous chapter at what may have been in His mind as He faced his immediate problem, so that we are free now to consider the import of His life for all time since then.

In this connexion, I am sure that we make a mistake if we suppose that from the beginning Jesus had a clear vision of all that would be required of Him, that He set out, so to speak, to put into execution a divine plan step by step. That would in effect rob His life of any human reality. Incidentally, the result is the same if we think of Him as governed in all His actions by some verse from the Old Testament which He was to fulfil.[9] He surely entered into life with the resolve to put Himself at the Father's disposal but with no clear knowledge yet of what that would mean. Did He not work at the carpenter's bench as one who saw in its tasks the sphere in which He was to glorify God? Those thirty silent years were not preparation merely, they were part of His self-offering and service. It may be that when He went out to teach and heal, it was with the confident expectation that His people would rally to Him and that the 'return' of which the prophets had spoken would be accomplished in His day. Then perhaps He saw that Galilee was closed against Him and went to the capital to meet a crisis which might involve His death,

[9] So, e.g. Hoskyns and Davey: *The Riddle of the New Testament* (1936).

E

though of this He was not sure. Only in the Garden did He finally perceive beyond doubt what His fate was to be.

So, as we do, He felt His way forward, spelling out word by word and even letter by letter, the divine purpose for His life. At any given moment He was ready to accept the Father's will in so far as He was able to discern it. And that will, He knew, was one which bound Him to His fellows, especially to those who were outcast from society and haunted by the rebuke of their own consciences. His place was with the sinner and with all who needed Him. So He took up into Himself an ever fuller measure of the divine will of love. Or rather, we should say, of the divine love in action. For 'will' might suggest no more than something intended, whereas what we are thinking of here is something actually *done*. It was only perhaps in Gethsemane that He fully understood what was required of Him and what it meant to be a channel through which God should enter the world in redemption. Upon that realization there ensued—can we doubt it?—a struggle of soul in which all that He had previously accomplished was imperilled. Having done the Father's will to this point, would He draw back from it now as something too awful to endure? He did not. With the prayer, 'Not my will, but thine', He took up God's action into His own without reserve.

Imagine that, starting from the same point, two semi-circles are drawn, so that to any point in the upper there is one in the lower which corresponds. Now the lines begin to draw together, one descending and the other ascending. But just as the upper semicircle is completed, the one who is drawing the lower hesitates and pauses for a moment. Will he desist and leave the work unfinished, spoiled even, or will he go on to meet the line which comes down to meet him? It was at such a moment that Jesus knelt and prayed in Gethsemane. And the line was continued, great as was the cost to Himself, so that the circle was completed and the love of God found that passage into the world which it sought by means of a dedicated human life.

This image may serve to bring out another point. God's will for His Servant was not something fixed to which He had to adjust Himself. He who respects freedom in the sinner would not override it in His Son. We must think of God's activity with Jesus as the shaping of His life from moment to moment by the persuasion of His wisdom, of God as enlisting His co-operation and training Him for the high tasks in store for Him. His manhood was a creation of God, not as something launched into the world ready-made, but as something which God brought to fruition through all His experiences. We may therefore say that Jesus Christ was the supreme act, the decisive deed of God for us men and our redemption. God came to us in Him. The strong, wise, patient love of God, waiting age by age to be gracious, was able through His dedication at last to come to us as it had always wanted to come. Not that God waited till Jesus was born to express Himself thus; He had always been endeavouring to do so, but only now was the opportunity given to Him.

Or we may say that Jesus is the incarnation of God's holy love. This it is, and not a mysterious divine 'essence' which takes flesh and walks among us as a man. Let no one say that this would mean that some impersonal attribute of God was incarnate in Him and not God Himself. For can any attribute of God be impersonal? And does not He who gives me His love give me thereby His very self? If the love of God suffers for me, I have the assurance of an absolute succour such as can never be forthcoming from any language of a divine substance which in its nature is not susceptible of suffering! The incarnation of God's love in Jesus is a gradual process and is conditioned all the time by the extent to which He enters into what God is doing with Him and identifies Himself with it. God's presence in Him is at every moment dependent on His dedication to God.

There are certain questions which may be asked at this point. I do not know that they all have meaning. For example, it may be asked how God's action in Jesus is related to that in other persons, since we have all along assumed that God is continually active. I reply by the analogy of an artist who has some vision of beauty he wishes to express and who finds, after he has expressed a part of it in this medium and another part in that, the material in which he can so convey his meaning that he is henceforth content. But it may be objected that such an account leaves open the possibility that God might one day find another human life yet more fully dedicated in which therefore His love would come to still fuller fruition. I reply that this is to invade the sanctuary with the ir-reverence of mere speculation. If a friend has given his life for me, I do not qualify my gratitude to him by the chill reflection that perhaps some day someone will do even more! In what sense, again, is God's revelation in Jesus Christ absolute? Not certainly in the sense that it is possible to demonstrate that it will never be surpassed. Even more certainly, not in the sense that we should look askance upon all new truth, as though Christ were a vested interest to be maintained against any threat from possible competitors. What can be said is that God in Christ so grips my soul that I yield Him unreserved allegiance, I want nothing more. But what I have in Him is not some-thing closed and completed in the past, it is something which accompanies me into the future, ever the same yet ever satisfyingly and surprisingly new.

IV RESURRECTION

The story of Jesus Christ does not end with the Cross. The Resurrection follows. Now, thanks to the Church's year, we are all so familiar with the scheme of Good Friday, Easter Sunday, Ascension, and Pentecost, that we find it difficult to think in other terms. That, however, is what a closer study of the New Testament compels us to do. For such study makes it plain that the scheme in question is taken from Acts and that other books do not reproduce it.[10] Thus, the early speeches preserved in Acts, as opposed to the editor's own view, do not interpose a time-interval between Resurrection and Exaltation. These are apparently two aspects of one and the same event. There is such an interval in John, but it is of the briefest duration. The evangelist speaks as though the Lord returned to the Father on the very day of the Resurrection (20[17]). If so, the appearances subsequent to that to Mary must be understood as appearances of the Lord *after* His ascension. That would explain how, in 1 Corinthians 15, Paul puts his encounter with the Lord outside Damascus on the same level as the appearances to the original disciples. In each case, it is the ascended Lord who manifests Himself in His body of light and glory (Philippians 3[21]). In his own theology, in the discourses, John goes farther and virtually omits the Resurrection. The Crucifixion and the Exaltation are the same event as seen first from man's side and then from God's. The verb 'uplifted' is deliberately chosen as having both meanings, and 'going to the Father' is something more than a euphemism for death. His dying is His return whence He came (13[1]). The writer to the Hebrews similarly has only one allusion to the Resurrection, and that in the benediction, which may

[10] The reading is uncertain at Luke 24[51].

well not be his own. In the book itself he definitely pictures Jesus as passing direct from the Cross into the heavenly sanctuary. There is no more room for a time-interval of forty days than in the ritual of the Day of Atonement.

We are therefore justified in saying that the New Testament writers agree on, and attach value to, one thing only, and that the conquest of death by Christ. And it would seem that for the deepest thought in the New Testament that conquest attaches rather to the Cross than to the Empty Tomb. In spite of all that has been said on the other side, it seems to me inconceivable that Paul in 1 Corinthians 15 would have made no mention of the latter had he known of it. The belief in the Resurrection is therefore the belief that the humiliation of the Master was by God's act His exaltation, that in the night in which He was betrayed He was glorified and God was glorified in Him. 'Faith in the Resurrection is simply faith in the Cross as a saving event',[11] as that victory over death by which we live here and now.

How then is the Resurrection to be understood? We may set out from the fact that for Paul it is not an isolated event in the past. It is something which is to be repeated in the experience of the Christian, both at his baptism and throughout his life. He must die with Christ and rise again. But where is the connexion between the ethical transformation of the personality in the present and what happened to Jesus after His death? It may be said that for Paul Christ is the representative of His people, or that they are mystically one with Him, or that, like the Gnostic redeemer, He includes them within Himself. All such categories are of the past and belong to a world of thought which we no longer share. That is true even of the mystical interpretation, if it is meant that Christ somehow carries men along with Him apart altogether from

[11] R. Bultmann: *Offenbarung und Heilsgeschehen* (1941), p. 66.

their consent. We shall return later to this question of solidarity and how it is to be understood. Here it is only necessary to urge a quite different procedure. Why not infer from the ethical character of the Christian's resurrection with Christ that that of Christ Himself was of the same order originally? Then the connexion between the two is a natural one and no problem is raised of how to effect the passage from a legal or spatial relation to a moral renewal.

Let us therefore make the attempt to take seriously the Resurrection as a spiritual experience and event. We can begin from the fact that the spiritual life maintains itself, not by seeking out favourable conditions, but by assimilating unfavourable experiences. The true man grows in soul-stature by what he is called on to endure. The frustrations and disappointments with which he meets are not allowed to daunt him, he so uses them that something from them is built into his personality. 'Sweet are the uses of adversity' in this sense. So was it with Jesus Himself; He grew by all that He encountered, whether pleasant or forbidding, in His service of God and man. And when He came to the last experience and the most painful of all, was it not so with Him still? We see Him in the Garden taking up into Himself the silence of God, the treachery or the cowardice of His disciples, the seeming failure of His cause, and all else that He was called on to endure. From this He emerges, collected and strong, to keep silence before His judges and refuse the kindly drug that would have dulled his pain on the Cross. So, we may continue, in the very instant of death, He assimilated, subdued to the gracious sovereignty and noble uses of His will, even that shattering blow. He took up death into Himself and passed on from it all the richer and stronger for what He had gone through. As others are made by the hardships they encounter, so He reached the dignity for which He was meant by the sheer horror and the resolute self-dedication of His dying.

We may say therefore that His obedience to the Father turned death itself into the supreme opportunity for His service, so that He emerged from it with a glory He had not possessed when He entered into it. We may, however, look at the same process from God's side. The writer of Psalm 73 used language convincingly suggestive of the faith that the God who had called him into His fellowship would not permit even death to sever their relationship. So we may say that God, having shaped the life of Jesus as the crowning expression of His will of love for men, would not suffer it to perish at the last. He who wrought it for so high a use would surely preserve it therefor. Nay, was not Calvary part of that divine discipline beneath which He learned obedience and became perfect as a Son? Did not God mean to make Him by death even more glorious and to act in Him by the Cross beyond anything He had been able to effect by His life? We must not connect the Cross and the Resurrection by some argument, as though the one implied that God had deserted His Servant but the other demonstrated that He had not. God meant the Cross rather as the moment at which His love should come to its triumph, at which it should meet with forgiveness and new hope even the rejection of itself.

The two movements of which we have been speaking go on beyond death, but they operate at a new and higher level. He who walked in Galilee becomes a spiritual personality who is with us to the end of time. God's deed of overcoming evil with good goes on with that personality at its centre.

The New Testament has recourse to imagery to describe this. It creates symbols to which we do grave injustice if we take them literally. When it speaks of the Ascension, for example, it suggests the attainment of a position from which an influence can be exercised which is exempt from the limitations of space and time and is as universal as God's dealings with our race. The exaltation of the crucified Jesus to the right hand of God means that henceforth that suffering, sacrifice, and triumph will enter into all our thoughts of God, that we shall know God truly not otherwise than in terms of them. Finally, when the writer to the Hebrews speaks of Jesus as making intercession for us in the heavenly sanctuary before God, we are not to suppose, as some of our hymns would apparently imply, that He induces God to be merciful by reminding Him of Calvary. The language means rather what I shall speak of later as 'the justification of man', the hope that blossoms from the fact that Jesus Christ is of our race.

When John speaks of the necessity that Jesus must go if the Spirit is to come, he is still using image and symbol. But their interpretation is now much simpler. The historical Jesus was of necessity a man of a particular country and period and as such He was bound to be a stranger in other periods and in other lands. He must therefore be liberated from that setting, that He might become a spiritual personality capable of entering into the experience of every generation of men. He who is to be with us always, even to the end of the world, cannot be quite the same as the one who was with Peter and James and John in Capernaum. What He was then must be preserved in its essential quality, the deed of God done in Him must go on. But what attached to Him as a child of His time must be discarded. The Man of Nazareth must pass, that the Spirit of Christ may come. For between the Risen Lord and the Spirit there is in the New Testament no final line of demarcation. The Pauline epistles indicate that as clearly as do the farewell discourses in the Fourth Gospel.

Is it possible for us to be rid altogether in this matter of image and symbol? I doubt it. For if we say, as one of my revered teachers used to say, that the things for which Jesus stood are seen to be of eternal value, we have not approached the heart of the New Testament faith and that faith which we can share with it today. In the last resort, the Resurrection is not what happened to the body of Jesus long ago, it is what He is doing today. I only believe in the Resurrection if I believe that Christ is still alive, that a personal relationship with Him is possible, albeit in a different way from that in which His disciples conversed with Him in the days of His flesh. Christ is still with us, He is the Great Companion on our road through life to the end of time.

> *Loud mockers in the roaring street*
> *Say Christ is crucified again:*
> *Twice pierced His gospel-bearing feet,*
> *Twice broken His great heart in vain.*

> *I hear, and to myself I smile,*
> *For Christ talks with me all the while.*

One has to fall back on poetry to express such a faith. Schweitzer does it in that memorable last paragraph of his *Quest of the Historical Jesus* in which he describes how Jesus enters our life today. Kierkegaard does it when he speaks of Christ as our Great Contemporary; even for our generation He is not past, but present. Any attempt to reduce the influence of Christ upon the world since His death to the power of His ideals seems to me pitifully inadequate; to speak of Him as still a living presence in our midst is alone equal to what is needed. And He is that by virtue of the spirit of self-forgetting service by which He conquered death and made it serve God's purpose in the very instant when He fell a victim to it. He is that also because the God who created and trained Him for sonship did His crowning work with Him in the hour when He seemed farthest from Him.

But how is Christ still with us? Is His presence immediate or mediate? The answer is that this is a wrong antithesis. I have an immediate knowledge of you, I know you yourself and do not merely infer you from your movements; yet it is by your movements of eye and hand and lip that you are brought into touch with me, mediated to me. If we say that we meet Christ thus in the Church, the language we use is so conventional and so liable to misunderstanding as to be dangerous. It suggests an organization with officials and stated services and so on. I do not deny that Christ may come to us in these, though it must sometimes be difficult for Him to do so. Equally, if we say that He comes to us in the preaching of the Gospel, the suggestion has too clerical a sound. Is it not better to say that Christ is with us in the devotion and fellowship of Christian men and women, the hearts He has touched and the lives He has moulded down the ages? Some of us have found His gracious presence in our homes, or in a small group of dedicated folk, or in one person who shines for us with unfailing radiance. A personal Christ comes to us first and foremost in persons and in the community which they form.

But this presence with us here and now of one who belongs to the past calls for further explanation. I suggest that two categories are needed, one modern and one thoroughly biblical. Jesus Christ is at once the *symbol* and the *deed* of God. By the use of these we càn do justice to the fact that in the New Testament Jesus Christ has the value of God, yet is normally differentiated from Him. He is Lord, while the Father is God. By the term 'symbol' I do not mean the sign of something absent, but a sign which effectually makes present. He is—I think the expression is W. E. Hocking's—'the human face of God', a life so wholly surrendered to God that we cannot worship God more truly than as we hold His picture before our eyes. The fuller our understanding of Him the deeper our discernment of God's nature and purpose. Devotion to Christ is the means to devotion to God. There is the ground of its necessity and the criterion of its legitimacy. In all this I would claim to be explicating what is involved in the New Testament statement that we worship God through Jesus Christ.

Then there is the second category, that of the deed. What has been said of Christ as symbol might suggest something purely subjective. It might indeed raise the question whether the value we find in Him is not, in the last resort, read back into Him by ourselves, as men today project on some political leader their own aspirations and make an idol of him. The deed belongs in the objective realm altogether. We may say that what God does for us men and our salvation is to express Himself again and again in and through the personality of Jesus Christ. Some fresh aspect of Him comes to light, some new claim is laid upon us by His teaching or His sacrificial spirit. The presence of Christ with us is not something additional to the presence of God, it is part of that presence itself.

Perhaps an analogy may not be wholly inadequate here. You have a friend who entered your life on one occasion by an act of such generosity as has made you for ever his. Henceforth, whenever you think of him, you see him in the light of that memorable event. Henceforth, in all that he does for you, he develops and extends what he did then. So God gave Himself to us once in Jesus Christ as nowhere else, since in His obedience unto death He found at last that by which He could express the self-giving which is His very nature. Henceforth, when we think of God, we see the light of the knowledge of His glory in the face of Jesus Christ. Henceforth, in all that God does for us, He shows Himself in ever fresh ways 'the God and Father of our Lord Jesus Christ'.

V SALVATION

One essential feature of the argument to this point has been a refusal to recognize the traditional distinction between the person of Christ and His work. What He is, is to be apprehended in and through what He does. We are now concerned to repudiate the separation between what Christ does *for* us and what He does *in* us. This means that we do not need to follow Anselm and add to our exposition of the Cross a final chapter showing how man's salvation follows on it.

The work of Christ is not an outward event to which somehow—by a divine decision which might have run otherwise, as a reward for His pre-eminent obedience, or by virtue of the Sacraments in the Church which He instituted—our salvation comes to be attached subsequently as an inward event. The two belong in the same realm. It is because what Christ did *for* us is ethical in quality that what He does *in* us is so also.

We can see this best if we attack the problem where it is most difficult. Perhaps the predominant imagery in the New Testament for what Christ achieved by His death and resurrection is that of a conflict with demon-forces. In our own day the attempt has been made to revitalize this whole set of ideas, notably by Karl Heim[12] and Gustav Aulén.[13] But it is doubtful whether they have succeeded. Yet there is something grand in that description in Colossians 2[14f.] of the Redeemer in airy combat with the hosts

[12] *Jesus der Herr* (1935).
[13] *Christus Victor* (1931). So now Chapman: *The Conflict of the Kingdoms* (1951).

of evil around His Cross. And clearly there was that in Paul's experience which answered to his language of Sin and Death as tyrants overthrown by Christ. Can we translate this imagery into our modern speech?

I think we can if we transfer the deadly struggle from the outer world to the inner. What happens in the soul is no less real than what happens before men's eyes. And in any case the encounter of the Lord with the demons was not for Paul a battle which could be observed and reported on. It was fought out in the spiritual sphere, which, for us at any rate, is in the soul. It was there, in the secret places of His own being, that Jesus faced the suggestions of temptation, that the expectations of His time solicited Him to go their way, that He questioned whether tradition was not too powerful to be challenged, vested interests too firmly entrenched to be dispossessed by one so weak as He. It was there also that death threatened Him with the undoing of all His work and delivered its assault even upon His faith in the Father who had sustained Him throughout life. The conflict was grim and the issue was not assured in advance. But Jesus emerged from it as victor. Yet the struggle was not ended so. For in that life which He lives among us still in grace and power He must contend continually against our pride and self-will, against the half-faith that would rather remain content with the status of a servant than go on to the freedom of a son, against the death that again and again breaks down what He has built up in us and in our world. 'The death that he died, he died unto sin once.' Jesus, that is to say, surrendered life rather than yield to the solicitations of evil. 'The life that he liveth, he liveth unto God' (Romans 6^{10}). He is now a victorious and wholly dedicated self.

As such, He marks a turning-point in history, He is the beginning of a new humanity. Paul states that quite plainly in his contrast between Adam and Christ. It is the obedience of the Second that has reversed the evil done by the transgression of the first (Romans 5^{19}). As a victorious and wholly dedicated self, with sin and death overthrown, Christ is a centre of power for all mankind. He can reproduce in us the pattern of His devotion, His acceptance of shame and death, and His triumph over these. We die and rise again with Him, because His death and resurrection were themselves inward events.

But how is this pattern of death and resurrection reproduced in us? By faith. But what then is faith? It is the identification of ourselves with Christ in His fidelity unto death, our participation in His spirit, our acceptance of God's will for ourselves as He accepted God's will for Himself. Salvation is by faith, not because faith is the condition attached to it, but because faith and salvation are two aspects of one and the same reality. To be saved by Christ is to be taken up into His sorrow for man's sin and His utter consecration to God's holiness. To believe in Christ is to begin this here and now by surrendering oneself to Him. The drama of redemption takes place in the soul of Jesus first and then in our souls. It passes from one to the other by the simple law that 'one loving heart sets another afire'. So we 'put on Christ', He is 'formed in us', we 'have the mind of Christ', we are in Him and He in us. These New Testament expressions are to be understood in a mystical sense, if that mysticism is through and through ethical. Devotion to Christ brings Him to the centre of our being instead of ourselves; we grow out of what we are hitherto into something so unlike it that we must call it by His name rather than our own.

As it is with the mysticism of the New Testament so it is with its conception of solidarity. There can be no doubt that the New Testament works with the Hebrew concept of corporate personality. It employs that category of 'participation' which is characteristic of primitive thought, according to which selves are not separated by sharp boundaries, but flow over into one another. Nowhere is that more evident than in John 17, where the fluidity is such that the Christian fellowship, the Son, and the Father are able to merge. Try as we may, we cannot think in these terms and think cogently. But solidarity is a fact with which we are familiar. Hence the attraction of theories which make Christ a representative Man, the archetype of humanity, and so on. Christ is so constituted that He, as it were, carries us with Him in what He does. But this is to employ the terminology of the New Testament to destroy its message. We participate in Christ only in so far as we identify ourselves with Him in spirit. His solidarity with us is ethical in character. It springs out of His will to identify Himself with us, to make our fate His own, whatever the cost. And our solidarity with Him, in its turn, springs out of, indeed is, our willingness to make His life and death our own, not as events that happen to us, but as transforming experiences through which we dare to pass, because He passed through them first.

There is a paragraph from Nicolai Hartmann which seems to me extraordinarily apposite to our discussion. I quote it: 'The vindication of man need not devolve upon all men. It may devolve upon the few, upon single individuals. Indeed it might devolve upon one only. Values are not diminished through the narrowness of the area in which they are actualized. A single individual can be the giver of meaning for a whole world, in so far as it participates in him. A life in which only one such exists becomes full of significance for everybody.'[14] We are familiar with the cynic's argument that so perverse a creature as man is much more likely to have come about by a cosmic accident than to have been intended by infinite

[14] *Ethics* (1932), II. 339.

intelligence. We have all had our moments when we despaired perhaps of other people, perhaps of ourselves. History raises the question whether the creation of man was after all worth while. The life that was at once crushed and enthroned at the Cross is the answer to all such doubts. Our race has not been in vain, since He has come out of it.

'A single individual can be the giver of meaning to a whole world.' Yes, but we must complete the sentence. 'In so far as it participates in Him.' And, as we have seen, to participate in Christ is not only to draw on Him for certain benefits but to be transformed by entering into His experience. All that He did and suffered must be sharpened to a point in *me*, to penitence for *my* sin, and self-abandonment to God's will for *me*. So I die to the old self and rise again to new life with God.

> *The Cross on Golgotha*
> *Can never save thy soul.*
> *The Cross in thine own heart*
> *Alone can make thee whole.*

VI   CONCLUSION

In view of the importance and the difficulty of this whole Christological conception, it may be as well to pause here and to summarize briefly the argument as developed so far.

We set out from a consideration of the relation between the divine and the human, suggesting that the divine fulfils itself in and through the human. It does so, of course, conditionally, since only as the human enters into the divine purpose can it become at all adequate to it. We saw that in Jesus and His Cross the divine forgiveness is uttered through human lips and the divine mercy enters

F

the world in and through a human self-sacrifice. And it was because Jesus shared so fully the divine attitude to sin that this was possible. The discussion in the present chapter does but carry the argument a stage farther. We see in Jesus Christ the highest instance of that divine use of the human with which we are concerned throughout. We see also how it is precisely by His obedience to the Father and His incorporation of His will into His own that in Him God Himself comes to us.

We can formulate the position thus far reached by saying that *Jesus Christ is the decisive deed of God for us men and our salvation*. Let us be quite clear wherein the novelty of this lies. It lies in the return to biblical categories as opposed to those of Greek metaphysics. Throughout the Bible the acts of God are the means by which He reveals Himself. As a personal God, He participates in history, and its turning-points are His deeds. So He acted in the deliverance from Egypt, and Second Isaiah is confident that what He did then will be overshadowed by what He is about to do in the return of the exiles. In the Synoptists, it is by acting in power, especially by His exorcisms, that Jesus manifests that God is with Him. In Paul, the Resurrection is the mighty act of God which can be repeated in the believer. In John, the death of Jesus in humiliation, shame, and agony is at the same time the supreme intervention of God in His world. We shall not err if we seek to continue for ourselves this line of thought.[15]

But it may legitimately be objected that if we have done justice in this way to one set of statements in the Bible, we have robbed others of their meaning. We have set Jesus in the sweep of history merely, whereas the New

[15] 'The revelation is best represented by the statement that Jesus Christ was an *act* of God—or, if one prefers, that in Him took place the revealing act of God.' Knox, op. cit., p. 29.

Testament context is eternity. It is now necessary to consider this objection in some detail.

What place, for example, does our Christology leave for *pre-existence*? Here we need to be clear of whom pre-existence is predicated. Not, surely, of the man Jesus, but of the eternal Logos. If that is so, then what corresponds to this in our conception is that the saving will of God which found expression in the historical Jesus was prior to Him and belongs to the very being of the Godhead. Of such a life as His we cannot think that it was a mere chance occurrence or that there was nothing more behind it than every other life. It is for us an expression in time of something that is for ever in the heart of God. If eternity is not that inconceivable thing, the time that was before time and will be again after time, if it is the impact of God Himself upon time, then Christ belongs to eternity as we do not. What came to us in Him was the ultimate divine intention, not something which began to be when He was born, but something in virtue of which He was born. He came into the world as the expression of the divine wisdom and love, and He grew up to achieve that which was with Him from the first. In that sense, we can agree with writers like P. T. Forsyth and H. R. Mackintosh that Jesus drew in His development on what was antecedent to that development. For, if we return to our earlier picture of the two movements and ask which of these was prior in Him, God's choice of His life to be the expression of His love or His choice of God to be His highest good, we must answer that the former was prior. He was what He was because God made Him such and He accepted God's work in Him, so making it His own.

Of the *Virgin Birth* little need be said. No special mode for the entry of Jesus into the world is required—we can think of Him as the child of Joseph and Mary and gain, it may be, by so doing. But He was none the less their child by an act of God coming to expression in Him. There is in the personality of Jesus an ultimate mystery, as indeed there is in every personality. None of us is explicable in purely human terms, there is a divine purpose and a divine hope in our arrival here. But there is between us and Him the fundamental distinction that in us that purpose is frustrated, in Him it was fulfilled. In Him the Word was made flesh and dwelt among us, 'the Word' being the dynamic energy with which God expresses Himself in act.

We may treat in the same way the assertions of the New Testament concerning the *cosmic significance* of Christ. 'In Him were all things created, in the heavens and upon the earth, things visible and things invisible, whether thrones or dominions or principalities or powers; all things have been created through him, and unto him' (Colossians 1[16]). That is to say, the will of God which became incarnate in Jesus of Nazareth and sustained Him upon the Cross is one with the will by which the world was made at the first. That world may at times appear confused and chaotic, a medley of contending powers rather than an ordered whole, yet there is nothing in it which will not finally be taken up into that patient, unwavering, sacrificial toil of love which was manifest in Him. True, we cannot reconcile the waste of nature or even its rigour with the self-giving of the Cross: we see not yet all things subjected to Him who bore it. But when we fix our eyes on Jesus crowned with glory and honour for the suffering of death, we have faith that all things will yet be His (Hebrews 2[8f.]).

But what, on this scheme, is left of the *Trinity*? It is best to be frank at this point. Of the Trinity as an account of the inner life of the Godhead nothing remains. That, in my judgement, lies in a region beyond any to which the human mind can penetrate. As such, the dogma of the Trinity is susceptible neither of affirmation nor of denial. It may perhaps be accepted on authority, though, since all authority is human to some extent, it is doubtful whether this can reach so far. It is sufficient to hold that God comes personally to us in His Son Jesus Christ, and that the Christ who conquered death and is with us to the end of the time can be spoken of either as the Risen Lord or as the Holy Spirit. The first name links the presence in our midst with the life lived in Galilee long ago, the second with the creative, life-giving energy of God for ever at work in the world.

This does not mean that the doctrine of the Trinity has no value whatsoever. As a rendering into concepts of the mystery of the divine being it is unacceptable, as a symbol it is fraught with profound truth. Its meaning then is that, whereas our life is torn continually between the claims of individual personality and social obligation, these two find in the Godhead their reconciliation. He is beyond their opposition as He fulfils in one rich and inclusive life those aspirations which for us are so divergent.

But when all has been said that can be said with sincerity, the question has to be faced whether such a Christology as is here set out can carry the weight supported by the one which finds utterance in our creeds and hymns. Will it move men with gratitude for an infinite divine condescension as the old belief in a God come down from heaven to die undoubtedly did? Now, no rendering of the mystery of Christ into concepts can ever grip and hold our hearts as the symbols of faith can do. One cannot in fairness expect the analysis and argument of a lecturer to do the work of the images which rose, fresh and creative, from the soul of an apostle. The test comes when one *preaches* such a Christ. And I trust that if one could only set before men this picture of Christ as the constant

Companion of our race, of life as the Emmaus road on which we walk with Him even when, alas, we do not know that He is at our side, of God as the Love that enters personally into our experience moment by moment, suffering in a concentration camp, hungering in a famine-stricken land, agonizing where a mother weeps over her wayward son—if we ourselves responded with every fibre of our being to a truth so splendid, then surely, even in this age of failing vision and ineffectual resolves, our words would not be wholly without power.

Chapter Four

Media of Revelation

THE ERUDITION and fervour of Karl Barth have combined to thrust into a central position in our thinking today the theme of the Word of God. That, as he has so forcibly maintained, is not what we say about God, but what He says to us. Nevertheless, it will be admitted on all hands that the Word of God only reaches us in and through the word of men. What God would say to us can only be heard by us as it becomes somehow an utterance on human lips. This applies not only to the Bible but also to the Church, its preaching and its Sacraments. A word spoken equally with a word written may bring to us what God has to say. Now, of course, a human utterance is, as human, subject to all sorts of limitations. It is fettered by that historicity which is characteristic of our existence in this world. That is to say, the word of man must be couched in some particular language, and this again is no merely conventional set of signs for purposes of communication. Every language has embedded in it the outlook upon the world, the metaphysic and the philosophy of life of a people. The Chinese language, for example, comes into the missionary's use saturated with Confucian ethics and popular Buddhist eschatology. So no empirical form of Christianity is without the influence of some tradition, some political institutions, some standards of value which are in origin pre-Christian. The modern Lutheran or Calvinist theologian who offers to the heathen the absolute claim of

87

God the Lord might have used other language had he not been living in an age of authoritarian régimes.

So much will perhaps be admitted on all hands. It is the next step which will excite criticism in certain quarters. But it seems to me that we do but reproduce the thought of the previous paragraph when we say that God's revelation only enters the world in and through some form of religious experience on our part. I know that to speak at all of religious experience is to ask for trouble. But is there not a misunderstanding on the part of our critics? There are, I think, three points which need to be dealt with.

In the first place, religious experience is not to be dismissed as purely subjective. There is no experience which is not experience of something or someone. What I mean by the term in this connexion is certainly not any set of pious feelings. It is an encounter with the living God.

In the second place, experience is to be distinguished from the fluctuating moods to which we are exposed and which may easily rob us of all security. My experience of my friend is precisely that deeper level of awareness which makes it possible for me to trust him even when his actions are not easy to explain and to maintain my sense of obligation to him even when, for the time being, I am not particularly attracted to him. The Psalter is full of this appeal from an incidental experience to an abiding one, and it is with the latter alone that we need be concerned.

In the third place, the accusation of rampant individualism is often brought against those who would appeal to religious experience. Are you not abandoned, they would ask, to the experience of one person, yourself, whether or not it accords with that of the race or the Christian community? This is the second mistake in another form. The basis of experience is whittled down till it becomes so narrow that little can stand on it. But the experience through which the revelation of God

reaches us is not that of any one person, it is that of the
whole company of His servants down the ages. To be sure,
we must not speak as though spiritual matters could be
decided by a majority vote, so that what comes to me as
the word of God can only be accepted after I have found
that it conforms to some generally accepted pattern. The
relation between the individual and tradition is of a different order. Tradition is not something alien to my inner
life which sits in judgement on me; it is a spiritual heritage
which I take over and assimilate. And the most personal
encounter of my soul with God is made possible by tradition and sustained by it. Yes, and even when I rebel
against tradition I must do so only in God's name, in the
name, that is, of its inherent truth against the forms it has
mistakenly assumed.

What is meant therefore by saying that revelation enters
the world in and through religious experience is that all
that we understand by religion, as tradition, as institution,
and as personal piety, belongs to that human utterance
which God employs to speak to us. This is part of the
language we use, the word we utter, and, like the language in the narrow sense of the term, it may convey the
divine intention to us or it may betray it and substitute
something of its own instead. The relation of religion to
revelation is therefore ambiguous through and through.
They cannot be separated nor can they be identified.
They may be two aspects of one event or they may be
mutually exclusive. And, of course, they may be in any
relation between these two extreme possibilities.

But if here, as elsewhere, the divine and the human are
inseparably associated, how are we to know when the
human is the servant of the divine and when it is its foe?
In other words, how are we to know when the word of man
conveys also the word of God? The only answer to such
a question is that revelation authenticates itself to con-

science. Conscience, that is to say, must decide between the various claims to be bearers of revelation. To discriminate between what in such cases is of God and what is not is its responsibility. This is no mere human arrogance, for the authority of conscience resides in it in virtue of its capacity of response to the holy and true. To steer by compass is not to impose one's caprices on the ship, it is to accept a direction which comes to one from beyond. So the discrimination which conscience exercises is not from itself but from the object with which it has to do. To be sure, conscience is not infallible. It is like the mariner's compass in that it is affected by all sorts of conditions. It seldom if ever points to the true moral north, but always is subject to some deflection due to social convention or personal training, or even prejudice. All that we can do is to retain the faith that there *is* a true moral north and do our best to find it by making such corrections as experience shows to be necessary.

There is, of course, a different and authoritarian conception of revelation. A very lucid statement of this may be quoted: 'The prophetic word is not something true in itself. In so far as the prophet utters things true in themselves, he is not a prophet, but perhaps a genius, or a sage, or something of that sort. But the prophetic word is valid because and in so far as the authority, the commission of God, stands behind it. The prophet says to me something which I am absolutely unable to say to myself. He says to me, if he is really a prophet, what God communicates to me as the absolute divine mystery, that which God Himself alone can know.'[1]

The inclusion of the words 'if he is really a prophet' surely vitiates the whole argument. What we want is some test by which we may know whether he *really is* a prophet; apparently there is no test. Nor does the description

[1] Brunner: *God and Man* (1937), p. 56.

appear to me to fit the prophet as we know him. The prophet as we know him uses analogies from nature and appeals based on history to lend force to his message. 'Come now, and let us reason together', he cries (Isaiah 1 18). In Second Isaiah we meet the argument from prophecy and a rationalist exposure of the follies of idolatry. Is it possible to read Amos and doubt that his was no mere *Deus dixit*? He had in the conscience of his hearers his best ally. The mark of that which is from God is not authority, but holiness, and conscience is that in us which is sensitive to holiness. When therefore the word of man convinces conscience, it is because in it and through it God Himself has spoken to us.

II THE BIBLE

It is another of the merits of Karl Barth that he has shown us the way to a dynamic conception of the inspiration of Scripture. The claim that we make for it must be couched in the present tense, not in the past. It is a statement of what the Bible can be for us here and now, not an account of how it came to be composed in the first instance. Of course, it will include that, but we must reverse the traditional procedure and move from the present to the past. If I take up the Bible and read it as one who is prepared to receive what it has to offer, I shall find that God Himself speaks to me through it. It becomes for me the place of revelation. I hear His voice calling me and reply: 'Speak, Lord, for Thy servant heareth.' The Bible thus becomes the word of God for me personally when the condition is fulfilled on my side. That may happen in some moment of illumination or conversion, as when Wesley was captured by a verse out of Romans. Incidentally, the fact that the same thing happened with Bunyan when words from Ecclesiasticus came home to him shows that the word of God is not to be confined to the canon. Or the influence of the Bible may be of a permanent and less emotional character, as a stabilizing force in one's whole life.

If now we ask to what in us this word from God in the Bible is addressed, the answer is that it is to conscience. We are not concerned, that is to say, with some sudden uprush of feeling or with some addition to our knowledge of the supersensual world, but with a claim to obedience and a call to opportunity and service. When God speaks to men He does so, not for their own sakes merely, but for the sake of the humanity to which they belong. Knowledge of God is of the practical order, not of the theoretical, and it binds us to our fellows by some mission that is laid upon us. The typical situation of call in the Bible is that in which a man is singled out to do the work of God on behalf of his fellows. It is with the great concerns of duty and responsibility, sin and penitence and forgiveness, that the Bible has to do. It has little to offer to the man for whom these mean nothing.

It may be said at this point that all this is true, but that it is true of many other books than the Bible, of the *Pilgrim's Progress* and of a modern book of devotion, of Marcus Aurelius and the Buddhist saints. Clearly, the cases cited fall under two heads. In the first instance where the literature in question is Christian, it can reasonably be urged in reply that the message which such books do unquestionably convey derives originally from the Bible. They are like the moon and shine by a borrowed light. In the second instance, that of non-Christian literature, while I would gladly allow that a veritable word of God may come to us from such a source, I do not myself feel that I should have met with God in the Buddhist and the Stoics had I not first met Him in the prophets of Israel and in Jesus Christ. What the result would be did I not bring to these books a conscience trained in the Christian tradition I simply do not know.

We touch here on a subject with which space does not permit us to deal. It is that of Christianity and the non-Christian religions. I will only say that I gladly acknowledge a revelation of God, a truth of God, in these. The Inner Light shines in every human heart since time began. The Christian view of God requires us to think of Him as always active and as always revealing Himself. I would distinguish between *the truth of God* as that which enters the world under many forms, some of them such that I cannot understand or appreciate them, and *the word of God* as that truth which claims me personally for Him. It is with the second we are here concerned, and it is this which comes to us in the Bible as we read it with a receptive mind and with willingness to obey what it lays upon us.

From this in the present we can argue back to the past. The Bible has significance for us in what we may call a situation of revelation and response. God speaks to us in it and we answer Him. Must we not then suppose that the Bible itself grew up in the first instance out of a whole series of just such situations of revelation and response? Those situations are not to be confined to the actual composition of the biblical books, they belong rather to the life of a community and of the individuals who were, so to speak, the centres at which what happened to that community was most vividly experienced and most faithfully interpreted. In the past, the word of the Lord came to a certain person, or, as Mowinckel would have us translate the Hebrew expression, it became a reality for him. [2] It evoked from him the response of obedience, he went out from the presence of God to subdue kingdoms or to work righteousness. Somehow, a transcript of that experience, that encounter of one soul with God on behalf

[2] *Die Erkenntnis Gottes bei der alttest. Profeten* (1941), p. 19.

of other souls, has come down to us, perhaps from the one who received the communication, perhaps from a disciple, perhaps only from someone writing down a tradition of it many years afterwards. But the thrill and splendour of that first-hand reckoning with God is preserved to us in the record, so that we who read it can enter in our turn, if we are willing, into something of the same order.

It is clear from this account as from what was said earlier that there is no opposition between the Bible as fraught with revelation and the Bible as record of religious experience. Here again we see the divine working in and through the human. God's self-disclosure and man's apprehension of this are two aspects of the same event. It only remains to draw out the implications of this position.

In the first place, it should be clear that truth in the Bible is always presented to us in a form conditioned by the historical circumstances under which it was received in the first instance. The heavenly treasure is conveyed to us in earthen vessels. It is not possible to pick out certain books or passages as from God and certain others as from men. Even in the sublimest and most convincing parts of the Bible there is something which stamps them as of a time which we have left behind and to which we cannot return. Even over against them, therefore, we must be critical at times, because what they offer falls short of God Himself. This is brought out by a study of the purpose of the Fourth Gospel. The writer claims to be led by the Spirit. He is disengaging the truth which Jesus brought into the world from the historical setting in which it came, so liberating it that it may enter into all generations to come. But does he succeed in arriving at a timeless truth? By no means. Indeed, his Gospel bears clear marks of the situation in which it arose. It reflects the controversies between Church and Synagogue at the end of the first century of our era, the struggle against Docetism and the followers of the Baptist. Even over against it therefore we must be critical, distinguishing between what is of God and what of the author and his time.

In the second place, what is true of the writers of the Bible is equally true of ourselves. We apprehend the truth of God within the limits and in the terms of our own situation at any given time. In an age of disillusionment we become attuned to features in the Bible that were strange to us in an earlier period of prosperity. We have seen in our generation how the eschatological element in the New Testament, dismissed once as mere husk, becomes later the very substance of the Christian message. The reason for the change is to be sought in the circumstances under which the theologian goes to work. His new insight is not necessarily truer than the old, it is more relevant to the time in which he lives, that is all we can confidently say. The word God speaks to us has reference to our concrete situation. Our apprehension of it is thus always limited, and we need to be critical even over against the faith by which we live. Our vessels too are but of earth, even though they may contain a heavenly treasure. There must be humility as companion of faith. What I receive of God is always partial and inadequate, because I myself am such. Yet it is from Him and I must follow whithersoever it may lead.

Let me sum up in a sentence or two. All revelation reaches us through some imperfect medium, and all response to it is from a conscience which is imperfect also. It is part of the discipline to which we are subjected that we should walk in the twilight and not in the noonday sun. Yet God has given us light enough to lead us to Himself if we are faithful to it. And what more do we need?

III   THE CHURCH

What now of the Church? The Church, like all that is human, belongs in that dramatic interaction between God and man on which emphasis has so often been laid already. There is an action of God, by which He seeks to achieve His purpose of good, and an action on man's part, which sometimes fulfils this purpose and sometimes frustrates it. What is unconditioned in God becomes conditioned in the world because a share in its realization is assigned to human freedom.

Once we begin to speak of the Church as of God, we find ourselves driven to go on to say that it is of man. And any statement as to its human character only does justice to it as it includes also a reference to that which is from God in it. Thus we may say, indeed we must say, that the Church is constituted by Christ. It is the sphere of His presence and influence. But how is this influence in fact exercised? If we take the Protestant view and say that Christ is with us in the preaching of the Gospel, is not that preaching a work of man? If we take the Catholic view, and say that the hierarchy and the sacraments are a continuation throughout time of His incarnate life, are not Bishops and priests human, and can sacraments be administered otherwise than through human words and acts? If the Church is the kingdom of Christ, can a kingdom exist without subjects? Nay, more, can it exist where they withhold loyalty? Christ is with us, even to the end of the world, in the community which witnesses to Him because it responds in obedience and devotion to His call.

We may say, in the second place, that the Church is constituted by the faith, hope, and love of its membership. Should these pass away, the Church would perish, for it cannot live on in a set of officials and the services they perform without being themselves inwardly committed to them. Yet do not faith, hope, and love presuppose the Lord who by His self-disclosure in goodness has won them? The Church therefore is at once His creation and ours. He only makes it as he draws us into His fellowship, and we only make it as we acknowledge Him as our Lord. The Church is neither let down from heaven nor a voluntary society for people with similar tastes in religion. It is one more place where divine grace works through human freedom; only here we have to do with a community and no longer with an individual.

Such a conclusion involves us at once in a rejection of that legal conception of the Church which is characteristic of Western Christianity, alike in its Catholic and its Protestant forms. We reject the formula: 'Where the Church is, there is Christ.' There are no external marks by which the Church is to be distinguished, neither the see of Peter nor the apostolic succession nor the preaching of pure doctrine and the right administration of the Sacraments. All these may be present and Christ Himself be absent. For they assure nothing more than outward conformity to a rule. One of the most orthodox sermons I have ever heard was delivered by a man who was personally an agnostic—he did it to oblige his audience! True, where faith is not, Christ may still be present. He is with us even when we reject and crucify Him. But there is no Church under such circumstances, for Christ has not that human medium through which He can express Himself. We must reject every suggestion that the Church is to be located elsewhere than where men and women acknowledge and serve Christ as Lord. Where that condition is fulfilled, He is truly present.

We need, I suggest, a radically personalist conception of the Church. We have said a thousand times that the Church is composed of people and not of buildings, but it is hard really to persuade ourselves that this is so. Our danger today is to become oppressed by an institution with programmes and budgets, secretaries and committees. But these are only the machinery of the Church, its life is elsewhere. Its life is wherever Christians meet in fellowship, wherever they 'know one another in that which is eternal', as George Fox put it. If a ship's company gathers for prayers on the high seas, if a mother draws her children to her knee and speaks to them of the Father in heaven, if a farmer and his man talk together of the secret of Christ as they milk a cow—are not these within the Church? On such occasions Christ draws near and is received, not by individuals as such, but by those who share a common life. Our conception of the Church must be generous enough to find room within it for every fellowship which centres round Christ. And by that word 'fellowship' I mean what happens when men and women are actually drawn together in Him, not some more or less organized group which may go on even after the inspiration which brought it into being has been lost.

The distinction betwen the visible and the invisible Church is a real one, though we have tended to grow shy of it of late. It is the distinction between the actual presence of Christ in a fellowship which He creates and maintains and a set of conditions which are designed to promote such fellowship. The one need not be pitted against the other, but the two may not be identified. I cannot assure another of my love without recourse to those fixed forms of language which are available whenever anyone feels a need for such expression. But those forms must never be divorced from the personal meaning, or they become mere conventions which falsify the relation between myself and my neighbour. So the mystery of spiritual communication between person and person in Christ needs for its health certain agreed regularities of time and place and even certain commonly understood phrases. The Society of Friends and the Salvation Army have recourse to these as does the Church of Rome. They belong to the visible Church, and we may say that the visible Church is the permanent possibility of the invisible Church, just as the Lord's Prayer, learned in childhood, is a permanent possibility of the approach of the individual soul to God.

The chief service which the visible Church renders to the invisible is that by its institutions it binds the generations together and preserves a fellowship which is not only with those whom one can meet in the present, but with those who have gone before. The Church is constituted by the dead as well as the living, since all live to God. In this respect the authoritarian type of Church has an advantage over others, inasmuch as it keeps alive the memory of founders and faithful ones in the past. Here what was said earlier of religious experience may be recalled. As we are not Christians in virtue simply of a mood which is here today but may be gone tomorrow, but by some attachment which remains however feelings may vary, so our faith is not our private discovery, it is our appropriation of something which has sustained multitudes of men and women before us. We need not seek for some sort of mystical communion with those who have gone before: we do not meet them as we meet Christ. But we are one with them as we share their faith and continue their service.

> *One family, we dwell in him,*
> *One Church, above, beneath,*
> *Though now divided by the stream,*
> *The narrow stream of death.*

IV   THE CHURCH IN UNITY AND DIVERSITY

We have now to consider what light the conception of the Church just reached throws on the vexed question of reunion. We differ principally in Church government and certain emphases which, without being susceptible to close definition, yet do mark off from each other certain fairly distinctive types of Church faith and worship. Let me begin with the problems of Church government.

It does not seem to me possible to follow those for whom Church polity is a mere matter of expediency. There must be a body which lends itself to the purposes of the Christian spirit. If the Gospel has implications for the life of society, it must surely have some for the life of the Church as a society. There must be therefore a form of Church organization which is of the *esse* of the Church. Nor should it be difficult to see what that is, if our account of the Church is correct. The unit of Church order will be the congregation, a group of men and women owning allegiance to Christ and seeking in all things to be led by Him. That is the conclusion to which Karl Barth comes in his pamphlet *Die Schrift und die Kirche*.[3] The individual congregation *is* the universal Church in that particular locality, because it is the group which the Lord of the Church has brought into being. It does not, of course, live for itself. It lives for Him and for other congregations, whether they are in the same denomination or not. Indeed, denominations do not arise in such a Church order as is here described. The local congregation is independent in the sense that it is directly responsible to Christ and may no more be overridden than the conscience of the individual Christian may be. It is related to other congregations in love and service, but not by any legal forms.

[3] See now *The Universal Church in God's Design* (1948).

There may be arrangements for the co-operation of congregations, by means of synods or other courts. But, as
Karl Barth rightly insists, these courts or synods must in
their turn be of the nature of congregations. It is only the
worshipping community which constitutes a Church and
we betray the intention of Christ in the Church when we
allow any court convened to transact business to take
precedence of a fellowship sustained by faith and prayer.

That, as I see it, is the type of order which follows from
the nature of the Gospel. It is of the *esse* of the Church in
the sense that the Church is not merely strong or weak, it
is present or absent according to the presence or absence
of such a common life. We cannot be too clear that an
organization of people to maintain a particular type of
Christianity by means of such measures as creed-subscrip-
tion has no right to the name of Church. It should choose
for itself some other description. The Church should at
all times be open, dangerously open if you will, to the
leading of its Lord, ready to prefer the truth to which
He bears witness in the present even to its most sacred
traditions.

It is not for me to say which among the existing
Churches comes nearest to the description I have just given.
I am quite clear that my own, the Presbyterian, cannot
make any such claim! We have all sinned and come short
of the glory and the simplicity which should have been
ours. Nor does it seem to me that anything is gained
either by seeking to create a Church after this pattern,
nor yet by leaving one's own for some other which seems to
come nearer to the ideal. In the first place, we do but add
one more denomination to the too many which already
exist. In the second place, we abandon the more urgent
and more arduous duty of working to bring the community
of our own upbringing nearer to what it should be. We
all live in visible and imperfect Churches; our task is to

make them more adequate servants of the invisible Church, the fellowship of those who share a common life in and with Christ.

There is, however, a second approach to this whole matter. The wide diversity of types within Christendom may be explained in either of two ways, as a reflection of the inexhaustible wealth of God's truth or as a result of the intractable self-will of man. The appropriate adjectives for the divine wisdom are 'manifold' and 'many-sided'. That is to say, it is so rich in nature that it requires for its expression a whole multitude of forms. Not merely do those forms differ among themselves, their diversity is such that for us they are sometimes incompatible and in conflict. We are not justified in erecting one single type of Christianity—always, of course, the one we hold ourselves!—as a norm and disposing of all others as so many perversions. The magisterial way in which Niebuhr, for example, dismisses Eastern Christianity and Karl Barth simply leaves it out, argues that such men are insensitive to ranges of truth which do not immediately commend themselves to their minds. The scholastic maxim that whatever is received is received after a fashion determined by the recipient's capacity may be cited here. It applies to God's disclosure of Himself, which is necessarily mirrored in each individual, each community, each civilization, and each period in history, in its appropriate way.

But our divisions are not due simply to the constraint which the infinite riches of the divine suffer when they are crowded into the little space of our human minds. As such, they would be inevitable and perhaps not quite so unhappy as we sometimes imagine them to be. They spring also out of such unlovely qualities in us as the will to dominate and reluctance to accept the restrictions imposed by a common task. What we may call the seamy side of denominationalism is exposed for us in a recent account of the separatist Churches in South Africa. Hundreds of Churches, most of them pitifully small and often with quite ludicrous names, have arisen, in the first instance to satisfy the needs of black men in a society in which power is a monopoly of the whites, and thereafter because some strong individual gathered his group around him to minister to his sense of his own importance.[4] What disturbing revelations might not be furnished by a study of the social and psychological roots of denominationalism in our own country? Are we quite sure that our traditions go back to principles rather than to prejudices?

If this analysis is correct, it follows that there are two possible paths to reunion. One of these we have been treading now for long, but it is difficult to believe that it will get us anywhere. Those who take it are severally convinced that the origin of their form of Christianity is in some principle which they must conserve, so that union will be a state of things to which each group will make its specific contribution. Is it not time we tried the second and more painful road? As we travel this, we must begin with penitence for our betrayal of the Master rather than with pride in our understanding and service of Him. If we could but face together the possibility that the things which seem so dear to us are dear because they symbolize our own ambition and self-assertion, not because they are God's gift, if we could but realize that the sin of self-will which the theologian detects in the individual and in the State is as strong in the Church as in them, what might not happen? A dose of Marxist criticism would do us all good. We might find that our doctrine of the Church was largely class-prejudice and our theory of the atonement a product of some vanished historical period to which we cling pathetically in memory because we were numerous

[4] Bengt G. M. Sundkler: *Bantu Prophets in South Africa* (1948).

and prosperous while it lasted. Is it not highly significant that the new orthodoxy, insisting as it does that sin must be made central to our thinking about man and society, declines to apply this insight to the Church? Karl Barth indeed began to do it in his *Romans*, but in his *Dogmatik* he speaks a different language. The Church is both the servant of the Word of God and a traitor to it. Once we are willing to begin our discussions of union from the second rather than from the first of these two facts, our goal will be in sight.

V THE PREACHING OF THE WORD

In one of his smaller books, Kierkegaard raises the question of how an apostle differs from a genius, Paul from Shakespeare, as we might say. The answer he gives is that the one is constituted by a natural equipment of some kind, the other by a supernatural vocation and endowment. The apostle is to be heard—here we see the origin of that view of revelation which we found ourselves unable to accept—simply and solely because he is a man clothed with God's authority. He partakes, man as he is, in the absolute qualitative distinction between God and man. For God has given him a mandate which he is to execute with His own authority. There is clear evidence that Kierkegaard would assimilate the Christian minister to the apostle. 'A sermon operates absolutely and entirely through authority, that of Holy Writ and of Christ's apostles.' Again: 'A priest is what he is through ordination.'[5] He possesses a *character indelibilis* of some kind.

Now this curious mixture of Catholicism and Protestantism is surely out of place in this context. Incidentally, was it ever more than a rationalization by which Kierkegaard

[5] *Journals*, 629, 716.

was able to evade the obligations of the ministry, after having been trained for it? The preacher is neither a genius nor an apostle. These alternatives do not between them exhaust the possibilities. Is there not also the servant of the Lord, whose mark is neither genius nor ordination, but dedication? The preacher, that is to say, is one who consecrates in all humility such gifts as he has received and such knowledge as he has acquired, and puts these and himself with them wholly at God's disposal, with the prayer that He will use them for His purposes as He sees fit. He brings to the pulpit all the preparation of mind and heart of which he is capable, neglecting no effort to understand his people or to state the truth in a form which will commend it to them, yet at the same time recognizing that the power to bring conviction is not for him to command. All true preaching is sustained by inward prayer. We offer our human utterance to God that He may speak His word through it. That God will use us according to our dedication is something we cannot prove. It is a faith without which He would be arbitrary and our service a chance.

There is an illustration here of our fundamental principle that the relation between the divine and the human is not fixed *a priori*. It is an open question whether I who am human will hold myself at the disposal of God or go my own way. If the preacher is neither genius nor apostle, he is still in good company. For is he not a lowly comrade of the prophet? It will be worth while to glance in passing at two interpretations of the experience of the Hebrew prophet. For Heschel, he shares in the divine pathos, the yearning of God over a people who have forgotten Him is reproduced in the soul of the prophet. These men 'felt the reality of the divine pathos with the same immediacy as they did themselves and their own sensations. That is what sympathy means, to feel the divine pathos as though it were one's own state.'[6] Mowinckel explains the sense of constraint under which the prophet suffers as the pressure of known duty upon conscience. The prophet 'bows his will under God and so must he do'.[7] His relation to God is a personal and ethical one, in which by faith, prayer, and dedication, he enters ever more fully into God's purpose with his life. I need not remind you at this point of how we found the key to Christology in just such a relation.

> *This is the way the Master went,*
> *Should not the servant tread it still?*

We are now in a position to see through the false antithesis implied in the question sometimes asked: Should the preacher draw upon his own experience or should he speak as a minister of the Church and a bearer of the Word of God? We have seen reason to deny that revelation and religious experience can be set one over against the other in this fashion. To save repetition, I will quote on this: 'God's revealing and man's discovery will not be opposite, but necessary, one to the other. God has not truly revealed till man discovers; and it is no true discovery unless it be what God has revealed.'[8] Substitute 'experience' for 'discovery' and the question with which this paragraph began is answered. When I speak of God I shall speak of a world of truth far richer than I have been able to apprehend, yet I may only speak of it because I have in some measure apprehended it for myself. To speak out of experience is to point men forward to something to which we have not yet attained, to bear witness to a reality we do not make but which makes us.

Nothing that has been said hitherto has been meant in a sense which would rob preaching of the mystery which

---

[6] A. Heschel: *Die Prophetie* (1936), p. 176.   [7] op. cit., p. 25.
[8] J. Oman: *Honest Religion* (1941), pp. 34f.

surrounds it. We do our best in study and prayer and all seems in vain; we speak a few broken words which leave us dissatisfied and someone is brought into touch with God. The dedicated soul is not necessarily the successful minister. How are we to explain these things? Quite simply, we cannot explain them and should not try to do so. In the terms with which Marcel has familiarized us, we must not turn the mystery into a problem, that is, into something which can be analysed, accounted for, and so disposed of, something which was to be expected to be like that. In resorting to such devices, we do but falsify the issue. We should see in the crises of our life-work, not just an unfortunate state of things which has to be accounted for, but a personal dealing of God with us. Our concern in His presence is not with the past, but with the future: that is the realm of His forgiveness, this the sphere of our duty. 'If thou return, then will I bring thee again, that thou mayest stand before me; and if thou take forth the precious from the vile, thou shalt be as my mouth' (Jeremiah 15^{19}).

VI   THE LORD'S SUPPER

Within the limits assigned to me, it is only possible to deal with one of the Sacraments. I choose as the more important the Lord's Supper, for Presbyterianism *the* Sacrament, as it is often called. It is necessary to say at the outset that, in my judgement, the evidence at our disposal will not allow us to think of Jesus as instituting, on the night of His betrayal, a rite which was to be continued by His followers for all time in commemoration of Him and His sacrifice. The Lord's Supper, that is to say, is not of Dominical institution. Granted that the words 'Do this in remembrance of me' belong to our earliest narrative of the last meal with the disciples and that the Synoptists can hardly have meant, by omitting the words, to challenge the current belief in the Church of their day, it still does not follow (a) that a specifically religious rite is meant as opposed to a meal of fellowship consecrated to the Lord, or (b) that the original command, if we suppose it given, had reference beyond the circle of those who shared in the Last Supper. There is, therefore, no obligation, derived directly from the Lord, attached to the Sacrament.

But does it follow that, like the Quaker, we should reject the Sacrament outright? I do not think so. Can one really approve the attitude of the monk in Whittier's poem *The Mystic's Christmas*? He sits apart from his fellows in their celebration, as they represent a stage in spiritual development which he has outgrown.

> *They needs must grope who cannot see,*
> *The blade before the ear must be;*
> *As ye are feeling, I have felt,*
> *And where ye dwell I too have dwelt.*

But now

> *The outward symbols disappear*
> *From him whose inward sight is clear.*

Is there not some touch of spiritual snobbishness in this attitude? And, without for one moment accusing Friends of this, is not the freedom of the spirit best revealed when one is neither dependent on outward signs nor averse from them, but can use them or lay them aside as the call of God may require? We can accept the Lord's Supper therefore as growing out of the Church's response to her Lord, a response which has seized upon and perpetuated under various forms the last occasion on which He had fellowship with His disciples. So doing, we shall rejoice in every opportunity to share this act of commemoration, worship, and witness, though we shall be equally ready to meet with Him where no outward sign is employed.

What has been said might indeed be expressed in more conservative language. I should be quite willing to endorse the judgement of Thèo Preiss when he says that Jesus founded the Supper, though by no legal act. 'He instituted it by His whole life, and especially by His death and resurrection.'[9] The same, he adds in a footnote, might be said of the Church. In each case, we have something which sprang naturally out of the impact of His life and work of His first followers, something therefore to be accepted with piety by us who come after them.

It only remains to offer a brief interpretation of the Sacrament in the light of that whole conception of the relation between the divine and the human which governs these lectures.

In the first place, it symbolizes the place of the material world in this drama of divine invitation and human response. A symbol, of course, is more than a mere pictorial representation of something. When appreciated and used rightly, it enables us to enter into the thing or experience symbolized. We should so discern Christ Himself in the service of remembrance, thanksgiving, and worship which centres round two material objects, bread and wine, that we may be able to meet with Him in all the transactions of life which centre round other material objects, be they coal or typewriters or books. I sometimes regret that deference to tradition requires us still to use wine at the Lord's Table even when we do not use it in our homes. Nor is it of any advantage when we manufacture some special wine to be reserved for this purpose. On the other hand, I have rejoiced, as a missionary, in the realism of the Communion service in a Chinese country chapel, when biscuit purchased at the village shop and tea from the missionary's cupboard were employed. The

[9] *Theologische Zeitschrift*, 1948, Heft, 2, 92; '*Le dernier repas de Jesus fut-il un repas pascal?*'

danger of making the Supper a purely religious rite is that it becomes formal and cut off from that consecration of the material universe in daily life which it is meant to teach us. Perhaps, as the Roman Church does, we should counter this danger by explicit instruction to our people.

In the second place, we see here how the life and death of Jesus Christ are the heart and centre of God's dealing with us, its consummation and its key. He so works at this specific point in history that we may see Him working at all points, above all in that contemporary situation from which we come to the Lord's Table. At the Supper, we stand at the point at which two time-orders intersect. One is the time-series in which we occupy a moment fraught with perplexities and regrets, happinesses and responsibilities, a moment in which, it may be, the world trembles on the edge of war. The other is that time of which I spoke earlier, in which the present is 'that complex of events which enters formatively into the making of our self-hood'.[10] The point we occupy in this is the 'night in which the Lord Jesus was betrayed'. That is the night in which men refused the one who was by right Lord of their hearts. Also it is the night in which He whom men had rejected so came, in and through His suffering, to His lordship. At the Supper we reconstitute that night of shame and triumph, we learn that our present hour does but repeat the shame and may, by God's mercy, reproduce something of the triumph. We live at once in this world with its problems and necessities and in the ever-coming kingdom of God. We see in the Cross and Resurrection the pattern to which we and the whole course of things are meant to conform, the pattern of victory snatched from defeat, of life born magnificently out of death endured.

In the third place, we see here how in this divine-human

[10] p. 41 *supra*.

drama which is our life, God meets with us in and through our fellows. Our communion with Christ at the Table is real only in so far as it draws us into solidarity with those who sit beside us. Again, Christ is present whether we acknowledge one another or not, but He is only efficacious as we are one in love. That is what makes so many of our communion services mere occasions for individual pious emotions and not at all the Lord's Supper. Stranger passes to stranger the bread and wine and we are no more a community than if we went, one by one, to kneel and receive them from the hands of an officiating priest. It is to a fellowship that Christ reveals Himself as it is through a fellowship that He does His work in the world. Some of us have very precious memories of a communion service in a small group of dedicated folk, meeting perhaps in peril and therefore all the more concerned to maintain the unity which might so soon be broken. At such times we have not doubted that Christ was in the midst. And when, under externally more secure conditions, we seek by suggestion and argument to revive a drooping faith, have not such memories guidance to offer us? Do they not whisper that if we were nearer to one another we might again be near to Christ?

INDEX